THE
JESUS
STORY

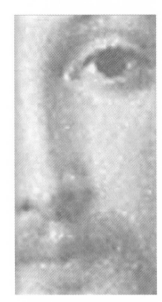

THE
JESUS
STORY

Ben Campbell Johnson
Brant D. Baker

GENEVA

Geneva Press
Louisville, Kentucky

Scripture quotations from the New Revised Standard Version of the Bible are copyright © 1989 by the Division of Christian Education of the National Council of the Churches of Christ in the U.S.A. and are used by permission.

The section titled "The Jesus Story" was first published as *Matthew and Mark* (1978) and *Luke and John* (1980) by A Great Love, Inc., copyright by Ben Campbell Johnson; reprinted by permission of the publisher. Original copies of this section may be obtained by writing to A Great Love, Inc., P.O. Box 1248, Toccoa, GA 30577.

Book design by Sharon Adams
Cover design by Terry Dugan Design

First edition
Published by Geneva Press
Louisville, Kentucky

This book is printed on acid-free paper that meets the American National Standards Institute Z39.48 standard. ∞

PRINTED IN THE UNITED STATES OF AMERICA
00 01 02 03 04 05 06 07 08 09 — 10 9 8 7 6 5 4 3 2 1

Library of Congress Cataloging-in-Publication Data
Johnson, Ben Campell.
    The Jesus story / Ben Campbell Johnson and Brant D. Baker.
        p. cm.
    ISBN 0-664-50117-6
    1. Jesus Christ—Biography—Sources, Biblical.   2. Spiritual life—
Christianity.   I. Baker, Brant D., 1958–   II. Title.
    BT299.2.J64 2000
    232.9′01—dc21
    [B]   99-056271

CONTENTS

INTRODUCTION

Who is Jesus? Have you ever wanted to know but were frustrated trying to find out? To begin with, there are four separate books about Jesus (Gospels) in the New Testament of the Bible; each appears to tell the same story, but with a slightly different arrangement of events. Additionally, in reading the Bible you encounter lots of strange names and places, obscure habits, and foreign customs. And in the story of Jesus' life and work is exciting "good news" about who we are and how we were intended to live. It is, therefore, no wonder that the modern inquirer gets confused and begins to feel inadequate in his or her grasp of the basic story of Jesus Christ.

The book you are holding is designed to help with this quandary in two ways. First, we have put together the story of Jesus in a seamless account that contains the material available in the four Gospels. The result is a story that is easy to read, thorough but not repetitive, and thus a way to get to know who Jesus is. We have used a contemporary paraphrase making the names, customs, groups of persons, and rituals of Jesus' day intelligible to a modern reader unacquainted with the Middle Eastern culture.

Second, we have provided boxed discussions beginning with "Consider Jesus Christ!" These are both introduction and invitation, exploring who Jesus is and what relevance he may have for us today. Here also, in smaller "Suggestion boxes," you will find interactive questions for reflection or discussion. Finally, the section "Questions People Ask" offers examples of personal questions you may be asking.

We are very much aware that, in one sense of the word, all of us are seekers, even those who have found. Followers of Jesus continue to search because no matter how long they have been following him, they realize that they are still beginners. There is so much to learn; there is so far to go—and we think the journey is fun.

But others are seekers in the most basic sense, those who are just beginning to discover who Jesus Christ is and what it means to be his follower.

Setting forth the Jesus story has been our effort to assist those persons in their quest to discover what it means to follow him today.

We hope this brief narrative of Jesus' life and accomplishments will answer some of your questions, stimulate your interest, and lead you along a pathway unknown to you today. Perhaps it will eventuate in your discovering who Jesus is in a very personal and meaningful way.

There are several ways to read this story that you may find helpful. First, you may wish to read the text through in one sitting. This immersion would give you a sense of the movement of the story. Or you may wish to read two or three pages each day and ponder what you read. We've divided the story into sixty days of readings. However you choose to read this story, we believe that paying attention to the various headings will assist you in understanding this person Jesus for today. Many of the headings offer an interpretive twist and propel the ideas from the first century into the twenty-first century.

THE JESUS STORY

‒ ‒ ‒ ‒ ‒

DAY 1

IN THE BEGINNING

Before the beginning of creation, one existed who expressed God's plan, purpose, and power. This one was in the very presence of God; in fact, he was God. The one of whom I'm speaking has always been in the presence of God. All creation came into being through the agency of this one, who encompasses the plan, the purpose, and the power of God. Apart from his agency, not one thing came into being. The one of whom I speak is the source of life, and the life that he imparts gives direction and purpose to all. The purpose he has implanted in humankind persists in the midst of meaninglessness and chaos, and the meaninglessness and chaos in human existence cannot conquer this irrepressible urge toward purpose and meaning.

The one of whom I'm speaking made his entrance into an existence that had its very origin in him, yet his own creation did not recognize him. In fact, he came to his own nation, to his own people, and they did not recognize or accept him. But some persons did, and these entered into a relationship with him. To them he gave the privilege of being God's children; these were the ones who trusted him for who he was. These who entered into a relationship with him experienced a spiritual birth. This was not a human birth or something they could create by their own power; nor was it anything another person could do for them. Rather, it was a birth that originated in God.

To put it succinctly: the one who expressed the purpose, plan, and power of God appeared as a human being and lived with us humans. We perceived fulfillment in him, the very fulfillment that God intended for all of us but made explicitly clear in this one person, who manifested unconditional love and the essence of reality. From the full expression of his being, each of us has received love, yes, unconditional love in each successive moment of our lives. Rules and regulations came through Moses, but unconditional love and reality have come through Jesus, the Christ. No human being has ever seen God. However, God's true Son, the only one God has ever had, is in the presence of God. He has shown us who God is and what God is really like.

JOHN 1:1–5, 9–14, 16–18

JESUS' EARTHLY LINEAGE

Here is the family tree of Jesus the Christ, the son of David, the son of Abraham.

Abraham fathered Isaac, and Isaac fathered Jacob, and Jacob fathered Judah and all his brothers. Judah fathered Perez and Zerah of Tamar; and Perez fathered Hezron, and Hezron fathered Aram. And Aram fathered Aminadab, and Aminadab fathered Nahshon, and Nahshon fathered Salmon. And Salmon fathered Boaz through Rahab; and Boaz fathered Obed through Ruth; and Obed fathered Jesse. Jesse fathered David, who became king of Israel; and then David the king fathered Solomon through the woman who had been the wife of Uriah. And Solomon fathered Rehoboam, and Rehoboam fathered Abijah, and Abijah fathered Asaph. And Asaph fathered Jehoshaphat, and Jehoshaphat fathered Joram, and Joram fathered Uzziah. And Uzziah fathered Jotham, and Jotham fathered Ahaz, and Ahaz fathered Hezekiah. And Hezekiah fathered Manasseh, and Manasseh fathered Amos, and Amos fathered Josiah. And Josiah fathered Jechoniah and his brothers at about the time that Israel was taken captive into Babylon.

And after the Jewish forebears were brought to Babylon, Jechoniah fathered Salathiel, and Salathiel fathered Zerubbabel. And Zerubbabel fathered Abiud, and Abiud fathered Eliakim, and Eliakim fathered Azor. And Azor fathered Zadok, and Zadok fathered Achim, and Achim fathered Eliud. And Eliud fathered Eleazar, and Eleazar fathered Matthan, and Matthan fathered Jacob. And Jacob fathered Joseph, who became the husband of Mary, who gave birth to Jesus who is called the Christ.

One way to arrange the family tree of Jesus the Christ is to recognize that from Abraham to David, there were fourteen generations; from David until Israel was taken captive into Babylon, there were fourteen generations; and from the time that Israel was taken into Babylon until Christ was born, there were fourteen generations.

MATTHEW 1:1–17

FROM BIRTH TO BAPTISM

When Herod was king of Judea, a certain religious official named Zechariah served in the order of Abijah. He was married to Elizabeth, a daughter of Aaron. Both of these persons were in a right relationship with God and responded without fault to God's guidelines and directives. The couple was childless because Elizabeth was unable to have children, and by this time both of them were past the age of childbearing.

It came time for Zechariah to perform the religious ritual. His particular function was to burn incense in the house of God. While he burned the incense, the crowd gathered and engaged in prayer. During his service in the house of God, he saw a messenger from God standing on the right side of the place where he burned the incense. The presence of this special messenger disturbed Zechariah, and he was filled with anxiety. The special messenger, however, said, "Don't be anxious, Zechariah. Your prayer has been heard, and your wife, Elizabeth, will have a son, and you will name him John. Because of his birth, you will be filled with joy and gladness. But many others also will be filled with joy because of his birth. This child will be recognized by the Lord in a special way, and as he grows up he will abstain from wine and other strong drink. And from the moment of his conception, he will be God-possessed. Because of him, many Israelites will return to the Lord their God. And your son will minister in the same spirit and power as Elijah. He will precede the Messiah, causing the fathers to be sensitive to their children, and those who are unresponsive to the Lord to learn from those who are. He will prepare a community of persons to receive the Lord."

"How can I believe all of this?" Zechariah asked. "You see, I'm too old to have a son, and so is my wife." The special messenger responded, "My name is Gabriel, and I am always in the presence of God, and I have been commissioned to tell you these things and to announce this good news to you. To validate my report, you will be unable to speak until all the things I've promised have happened. This particular sign was chosen because you did not believe my message."

Those people who were praying outside waited a long time for Zechariah, and they were amazed at the length of his stay. When he finally emerged, he was unable to speak. The people concluded that he had seen a vision in the house of God. He was able to make signs and motions but was speechless. When his time of service in the house of God was completed, he went home.

After that, Elizabeth became pregnant and went into seclusion for five months. Elizabeth celebrated by saying, "In my old age, the Lord has blessed me and has removed any cause for others to reject me."

LUKE 1:5–25

DAY 2

JESUS' BIRTH ANNOUNCED

When Elizabeth was six months pregnant, Gabriel, who had appeared to Zechariah, was sent by God to Nazareth, a city in Galilee. He went to Mary, a virgin engaged to Joseph, a descendant of David. The special messenger met her, saying, "Greetings! You have been especially chosen. The Lord is with you in a special way." This greeting baffled her, and she was filled with anxiety and wondered what it meant. Then the messenger said, "Don't be anxious, Mary, for you have found a special place with God. I have come to announce that you will conceive a son and give birth to him. And you are to name him Jesus. He will be a remarkable son and will be recognized as the Son of God, and God will make him a ruler of the people like his father David before him. He will rule over the people always, and his rulership will be unending."

Mary asked, "How will this happen, since I have not had intercourse with a man?"

The special messenger replied, "The Holy Spirit will act on you, and the presence of the Creator will touch you; thus, the child you bear will be called the Son of God. Already your cousin Elizabeth, even in her old age, has conceived and is six months pregnant. I tell you of that because nothing is impossible with God."

Mary acknowledged simply, "Consider me the servant of the Lord, and let it happen to me according to your prediction." Then the special messenger departed.

LUKE 1:26–38

When he discovered her pregnancy, Joseph, Mary's fiancé, being a compassionate person, did not wish to embarrass her publicly, so he was con-

Consider Jesus Christ!

Consider him as a present reality to know, respect, and follow. Consider him as an answer to the confusion and violence rampant in the modern world. Consider him as the one who can give meaning to our lives in the midst of our personal and national chaos.

Could it be that one who came so long ago to show us the way of peace, the way of meaning, the *(continued)*

Suggestion #1

Before you begin reading this text, make a list of all the things you believe or don't believe about Jesus.

sidering breaking their engagement quietly. While he was dealing with his conflicting feelings, he had a dream that clarified his decision. In the dream, a special messenger of God appeared to him and said, "Joseph, David's son, do not be anxious about your engagement to Mary. Take her for your wife, because the child she has conceived is a result of the action of the Holy Spirit. She will give birth to a son whom you are to name Jesus, because he will liberate his people from all that oppresses them." These events took place to fulfill what one of the Lord's spokespersons had said long ago: "One day, a virgin will be pregnant and will bear a son, and his name will be called 'God with us.'" When Joseph awoke, he did as the Lord's special messenger in the dream had instructed, and he married Mary. But Joseph did not have intercourse with Mary until the baby was born; and as was instructed, he called his name Jesus.

MATTHEW 1:19–25

About that time, Mary left Nazareth and went with haste into the countryside to the town in Judea where Zechariah lived. She went immediately into his house and greeted Elizabeth. At the moment of Mary's greeting, the baby in Elizabeth's womb gave a hard kick, and she was filled with the Holy Spirit. Elizabeth declared, "You have been chosen from all the women in the world, and the baby in your womb has been chosen, too. And what will I do because the mother of my Lord has come to visit me? Why, when I heard your greeting, the baby in my womb kicked and jumped for joy. You are certain to be fulfilled because you have trusted God's promise, and you have done the things that the Lord instructed you to do."

Mary responded, "My inner being worships the Lord. My spirit is rejoicing in God, my Savior. God has recognized the humility of God's servant, and in the future all persons will recognize my fulfillment. The

---

way of life—could it be that this one who has endured the ages—actually answers the deepest questions of our age and all the ages?

Many in the modern world have ignored the exemplary life of Jesus, the simple but profound teaching he did, and the amazing fact of his rising from death. We believe that many have ignored him because of false assumptions about him or because of hearsay comments that represent him as irrelevant for us today. Do you actually know what he said? What he did? What his own companions said about him? You can find out firsthand if you are willing to embrace a bit of intellectual honesty.

(continued)

powerful one has done marvelous things for me, and God is to be reverenced. God's tenderness and forgiveness are expressed to those who reverence God from one generation to another. The Holy One has revealed God's mighty strength. God has divided the boastful through their wild fantasies. God has removed the strong from their thrones of power and replaced them with humble persons. God has given the hungry everything they wanted to eat, and God has dismissed the wealthy empty-handed. The Holy One has responded to the chosen people, because they remember that God is tender and kind. God made a promise to our fathers, even to Abraham, and to his descendants forever."

LUKE 1:39–55

DAY 3

THE BIRTH OF JOHN

Mary stayed with Elizabeth for about three months and returned home. After her departure, Elizabeth gave birth to a son. Everyone around—her neighbors, kin, and others—recognized God's love and tenderness and celebrated with her. On the eighth day, they circumcised the infant and were going to name him Zechariah after his father. But his mother responded, "No, he is to be named John." All those gathered for the celebration said, "You don't have any relatives named John." Then they signaled to Zechariah, asking what name the child was to have. He requested a writing pad and wrote, "His name is John." Everyone there was amazed. At that moment, Zechariah's speech returned, and he praised and worshiped God. Everyone was filled with awe. Later, they told throughout the hill country of Judea what had happened. And all those who heard the report wondered

---

Some time ago, one of us met a man who professed to be an agnostic. He held that Jesus was a figment of the human imagination, that the church had embellished Jesus' story in order to control the powerless, and that religion was an anesthetic to dull the pain of daily living. One day, however, it occurred to him that he did not know anything about Jesus. He had never exposed himself to the life and teachings of Jesus as they are preserved in the Bible.

With a degree of excitement, he began to describe his experience of his first exposure to Jesus. He said, "I began reading the Bible as an act

(continued)

---

in their hearts, "What kind of child will this be? God's presence is with him in a special way."

LUKE 1:56–66

ZECHARIAH'S PREDICTION

At this time, Zechariah was filled with the Holy Spirit and offered this prediction: "May the Lord God of Israel be fulfilled because God has come to God's people to bring them back into a relation with God. The Holy One has given to us the announcement of healing and wholeness through the image of David. Ever since the beginning of time, God has forecast through his spokespersons that we would be delivered from our enemies and from all those who reject and persecute us. The Lord will now show the tenderness and kindness promised to our fathers in the covenant with them. God will honor the promise given to our father Abraham and will now give us the opportunity to worship God without anxiety by delivering us from our enemies. Let us live in reverence and right relations before God always. And you, my son, will be a spokesman for God. You will precede the Holy One to prepare for his ministry. You will announce healing to all persons, promising them the forgiveness of their sins. Through the kindness and forgiveness of our God, the source of life and light has appeared in our midst to shine on those who are in darkness, living under the shadow of death, and to direct us into peace."

And in due course, the child developed and became strong in spirit. He later withdrew into the desert, waiting until the time he should appear to the Jewish people.

LUKE 1:67–80

---

of intellectual honesty. I admitted to myself that for years I had been skeptical about the Bible, but all my reactions were based on the opinion of others. I had never personally read the text. In the name of intellectual integrity, I decided to read the story of Jesus for myself."

As he read the story of Jesus, something began to happen to his misguided assumptions. He began to see Jesus in a new light, not as a deceiver of the people, a charlatan, but as a humble servant to those in need. In the narrative of Jesus' life, he met a man of principle, one who stood firm in the face of death. The man he met in the story challenged

(continued)

DAY 4

JESUS' BIRTH

About the time John was born, the Roman ruler, Caesar Augustus, issued an order that everyone under his rule should be enrolled in a census. (The census was taken in Israel when Quirinius was overseeing Syria.) And everyone went to his place of birth to be enrolled. Because Joseph was a descendant of David, he went up from the city of Nazareth into Judea and came to Bethlehem, which is David's city of origin. His purpose was to be enrolled in the census with Mary, to whom he was engaged and who by this time was far along in her pregnancy. While they were there for the enrollment, the time came for her baby to be born. And she gave birth to her child, a son, and wrapped him in the clothes of a newly born and placed him in a trough from which the animals ate. He was born in a barn because the inn was full.

LUKE 2:1–7

SHEPHERDS HEAR THE GOOD NEWS

In that region around Bethlehem were a number of flocks of sheep whose shepherds stayed with them in the fields during the night. A special messenger from God appeared to a group of these shepherds, and when the presence of God was manifested to them, they were very frightened. The messenger said, "Don't be afraid. Listen to me. I have good news for you. It will cause you and everyone else to rejoice. For your sake, on this very day in Bethlehem, where David came from, the deliverer has been born— the Messiah who is the Lord. You will recognize this special child because he will be wrapped in strips of cloth and lying in a feed trough." And with

---

him, inspired him, and directed his steps along new pathways. Christ became a living reality in his life. The smile on his face told more than his words of witness. He was, indeed, a man on the way to life.

In this edition of the story of Jesus, compiled from sources that have been around for nearly 2,000 years, we have prepared a way to hear the original story of Jesus. He's worth considering. The following quote underscores the significance of Jesus for human history, as well as his significance for us today.

(continued)

that announcement, the sky seemed to be filled with a choir singing and worshiping God, saying, "Glory to God in the highest, and peace to all God's people."

When these heavenly messengers departed, the shepherds marveled at their announcement. Finally, one spoke: "Let's go into Bethlehem and see for ourselves what's happening." Because of their excitement, they made the trip quickly. Just as the announcement said, they found Mary and Joseph in a stall and the baby lying in a feed trough. After the shepherds verified the announcement for themselves, they began telling people everywhere. All their hearers were awed by the story the shepherds told. Mary, however, did not tell the stories to everyone; she retained them in her memory and meditated on them in her heart. And the shepherds went back to their flocks worshiping and praising God because of all the things they had experienced.

When the child was eight days old, he was circumcised according to the Jewish custom. And they named him Jesus, because of the messenger's instruction to Mary before he was conceived.

LUKE 2:8–21

SIMEON AND ANNA HONOR JESUS

Jesus' parents waited another month after the circumcision before taking him to Jerusalem, to dedicate him to the Lord and to have Mary purified. This dedication was also in accordance with the rules Moses had received, which said, "Every male child that is born will be especially dedicated to the Lord." Part of the dedication of the child was the offering of a sacrifice; in this instance, the sacrifice was a pair of doves, or two pigeons.

> For over a thousand years . . . he dominated the culture of the West: its religion and devotion, its art, music, and architecture, its intellectual thought and ethical norms, even its politics. Our calendar affirms his life as a dividing point in world history. On historical grounds alone, with no convictions of faith shaping the verdict, Jesus is the most important figure in Western (and perhaps human) history. . . . Thus, simply as a matter of intellectual or historical curiosity, it is interesting to ask, "What was this towering cultural figure like as a historical person
>
> *(continued)*

The Jesus Story

In Jerusalem lived a good man, dedicated to God, who expected to see Israel's Messiah. His name was Simeon, and the Holy Spirit was in his mind and heart in a special way. The Holy Spirit had already shown Simeon that he would not die before he had seen the Messiah. He was often led by the Spirit into God's house. When the parents of Jesus brought their son there in obedience to the rules, Simeon took the child in his arms and worshiped God. He then said, "Lord, your servant can now die willingly because your word to me has been fulfilled. I have seen for myself the way you will bring healing and wholeness not only to Israel, my nation, but to everyone. This gift of yours will bring direction and meaning to non-Jews and also to your people Israel."

Both Joseph and Mary were amazed at what Simeon said. Then Simeon laid his hands on them and prayed for them and said to Mary, "Your child will have a great impact on Israel. Many will draw nearer, and others will depart, and still others will attack him. Indeed, your own heart will be broken as if a sword is thrust into it, but he will also expose the thoughts and motives of many hearts."

Also in God's house was a woman named Anna, a spokesperson for God. Her father was Phanuel of the tribe of Asher. She was a very old woman who had lived with her husband seven years until he died and then alone until she was eighty-four. She never left God's house but spent her time worshiping God day and night with fasting and prayer. About this time she came into God's house and immediately began giving thanks to the Lord, and she spoke about Jesus to all of those who were expecting the deliverance of Jerusalem.

LUKE 2:22–38

---

before his death? (Marcus Borg, *Jesus: A New Vision: Spirit, Culture, and the Life of Discipleship*, San Francisco: Harper, 1987, p. 1.)

A person of this stature certainly demands consideration as a model or noble example, if nothing else.

• You may be a person who has grown up in the North American culture where the name of Jesus was spoken

(continued)

DAY 5

VISITORS FROM THE EAST

The king at that time, King Herod, heard of Jesus' birth when a traveling party of astrologers from the East came to Jerusalem. They inquired, "Where is the one who has been born to rule the Jews? We have seen an unusual configuration of stars in the East and have come to pay our respects to him." The reported birth of a ruler caused Herod to be anxious; in fact, the whole city shared his distress. The troubled Herod gathered the religious leaders as well as the interpreters of the rules, and he inquired of them where the Christ was to be born. Without hesitation they said, "In Bethlehem of Judea, because one of our spokespersons has said, 'And you Bethlehem, in the land of Judah, are not inferior to any of the princes of Judah, because from you shall come a leader who will govern all the people of Israel.'"

After his conference with the leaders, Herod held a private meeting with the astrologers and asked them at what specific time they had seen the astral configuration. At the conclusion of their conference, Herod dispatched them to Bethlehem saying, "You go and search high and low for this child. When you have found him, bring me a report so that I may pay my respects to him also." With that word from the king, the astrologers departed. To their amazement, the star they had seen in their own country appeared again and guided them directly to the baby. The reappearance of the phenomenon in the heavens overjoyed them. The astrologers entered the house and found the baby with Mary, his mother. They fell to their knees to worship, opened their bags, and offered gifts: gold, incense, and spices. After seeing the baby, the astrologers had a dream in which God

---

but not understood. Take this opportunity to consider some more about Jesus Christ.

• You may have been reared in a culture that had a different basis for a religious life. Even so, we invite you to consider Jesus Christ.

• You may have been on the margin of a church, hearing and speaking the name of Jesus Christ with regularity but without any depth of conviction or commitment to

(continued)

---

instructed them not to report back to Herod but to return to their homes by another route.

MATTHEW 2:1–12

HEROD'S CRUEL DEED

One of God's special messengers spoke again to Joseph in a dream, saying, "Get up and take the baby and his mother and go into Egypt. Stay there until I call you to return, because Herod will endeavor to destroy the child." Joseph got up during the night and departed with his family for Egypt. They remained there until the death of Herod, so that the ancient prediction could be fulfilled that said: "Out of Egypt I have called my son."

After Herod had waited a number of months for the return of the astrologers, it became obvious to him that they would bring him no information concerning the birth of Jesus. Insane with anger, he sent his soldiers into Bethlehem and the surrounding countryside with instructions to kill all the male children two years old and under. His calculation concerning the child's age was based on the time that the astrologers had first visited him. This act also concurs with what the ancients had predicted would happen. God's spokesman Jeremiah said, "In Ramah, there was heard a loud voice of weeping and crying and deep mourning. Rachel, a mother, wept for her children and would let no one comfort her because they were all taken away."

When Herod died, a special messenger of the Lord again spoke to Joseph in a dream, while he was living in Egypt. The messenger said, "Get up and take your son and his mother and go back into the land of Israel, because the king who sought to destroy him is dead." So Joseph got up, took the boy and his mother, and came back to his native land of Israel. On

---

his way of life. Would it not be helpful for you to reconsider JesusChrist?
- You may be one of those who has heard the story of Christmas and Easter for a long time, but with little significance beyond new clothes and presents. Again, it may be helpful for you to reconsider Jesus Christ.
- Perhaps you are like the person described in the hymn: "I love to tell the story . . . for those who know it best

(*continued*)

his arrival, he heard that Archelaus, Herod's son, was governing the land in the place of his father. This news frightened Joseph, but once again God spoke to him in a dream, instructing him to depart into Galilee. So Joseph settled in the town of Nazareth. This decision had been predicted by one of the ancients, who said, "He shall be called a Nazarene."

MATTHEW 2:13–23

AN EARLY SIGN OF JESUS' IDENTITY

Every year, Jesus' parents went to Jerusalem to celebrate the Jews' deliverance from Egypt. When he was twelve years old, a memorable incident occurred during this Passover in Jerusalem. They had finished their stay and started home, but the child, Jesus, stayed in Jerusalem. Joseph and Mary didn't know about this, so they traveled a full day thinking he was in the crowd. Then they began looking for him among their relatives and friends. When they could find neither Jesus nor anyone who knew anything about him, they went back to Jerusalem to search for him. Three days later they discovered him in God's house, sitting in the midst of the teachers of the law. He was both hearing their explanations and asking them questions. Everyone who heard his conversation with these learned persons was astonished at his comprehension and his responses. His parents were shocked when they saw him, and his mother said, "Son, why have you done this to us? Don't you know that your father and I have been disturbed and anxious?" He responded to them, "Why did you spend so much time looking for me? Didn't you realize that you would find me in my Father's house?" They didn't understand what he meant. He went back with them to Nazareth and was responsive to their instructions. Again, his mother retained this experience in her memory and pondered it in her heart. And

seem hungering and thirsting to hear it like the rest!" For you to consider Jesus Christ would be to consider him in new depth with greater understanding.

Jesus matured both physically and mentally and grew in his relationship with others and with God.

LUKE 2:41–52

DAY 6

JOHN PREPARES THE WAY FOR JESUS

Here is the setting for the beginning of Jesus' ministry. During the fifteenth year of the rule of Tiberius Caesar, Pontius Pilate was governor of Judea, Herod Archelaus was tetrarch of Galilee, Herod's brother Philip was the tetrarch of Ituraea and of Trachonitis, and Lysanias was the tetrarch of Abilene. Annas and Caiaphas were the high priests for the year. At that time, God called to John, the son of Zechariah, who was out in the desert. In response to the call, John went into the region around the Jordan River and began preaching that persons should change their attitudes and behavior and be baptized for the forgiveness of their sins. Isaiah, the spokesman of God, had written: "A voice crying in the desert, 'Make way for the Lord, level the ground before him. All the valleys will be filled up, and all the mountains and hills will be leveled out, and the crooked roads will be straightened, and the rough roads will be made smooth. And everyone shall see the Savior sent from God.'"

LUKE 3:1–6

Now, John lived as an ascetic. He wore a vest of camel's hair and a leather belt. He ate the fruit of the locust tree mixed with wild honey. Both his witnessing and his strange manner of life attracted crowds from Jerusalem and the whole countryside of Judea around the river Jordan. Many of those who listened to his testimony submitted themselves to his baptism and

---

We invite you to consider Jesus seriously as one who defines the way to live our lives on this earth and as one who shows us how human beings are related to God. We are certain that in this short essay we will not answer all your questions about the person of Jesus Christ. Nor will we offer irrefutable proof of Jesus' and Christianity's superiority over other religions. We will not delve into the historical accuracy of the sayings of Jesus, nor will we exam-

Suggestion #2

As you reflect on these possible perspectives, which best describes your own place of beginning?

---

acknowledged the sinfulness of their attitudes and actions.

MATTHEW 3:4–6

John addressed the crowd who had come to be baptized by him, "You are a bunch of snakes! Who told you to get ready for the catastrophe that is coming? Demonstrate by your lives that you have really changed your attitude. And don't rationalize, saying, 'My father is Abraham.' I tell you, God can turn these lifeless stones into children of Abraham. The ax is already hacking away at the root of your tree, and every tree that does not produce good fruit will be cut down and used for firewood."

The crowd asked him, "What kind of change in behavior do you mean?" He said, "If you have two coats, give one to a person who is coatless, and if you have more food than you need, share with the hungry." The tax collectors approached him for baptism and asked, "Teacher, what change do you want from us?" He responded, "Don't collect more taxes than you are supposed to." Then the soldiers asked, "What change do you demand in us?" And he said to them, "Don't harm anyone; don't lie about anyone; and be satisfied with the salary you are making."

Since there was a growing air of expectancy among the people, many of them secretly wondered whether John was the Messiah. John responded to their question by saying, "I am baptizing you with water, but one is coming who is superior to me, whose shoes I am not worthy to untie. He will immerse you in the Holy Spirit and will set your hearts on fire. He holds a separator in his hand with which he will fan away the chaff of your lives and will preserve the wheat. He will gather the wheat into the granary and he will burn the chaff."

LUKE 3:7–17

DAY 7

JESUS IS BAPTIZED

Sometime after the John the Baptizer's pronouncement to the religious leaders, Jesus came from his home in Galilee to Judea to that region of the Jordan where John was baptizing. He asked John to baptize him. John was appalled at Jesus' request and resisted him, saying, "I really need to have you baptize me. Why do you ask me to baptize you?" Jesus responded, "Go ahead and baptize me, John, because I must fulfill God's purpose by identifying with all the people."

At this, John baptized Jesus. The baptism was a peak experience for Jesus. After John had administered the baptism, Jesus came immediately out of the water and heaven was opened up to him, and the very Spirit of God came upon him like a dove flying through the sky. And in that ecstatic moment, he heard a voice from heaven saying, "You are my much-beloved son; I am very pleased with you."

MATTHEW 3:13–17

ENCOUNTER WITH THE ADVERSARY

Returning from the Jordan full of the Holy Spirit, Jesus was led by the Spirit into the desert to be tested by the Adversary. To prepare for this testing, Jesus abstained from food and drink for forty days, and after that he was hungry. Then the Adversary came to him with the first test: "If you really are the Son of God, as the voice said at your baptism, transform this rock into food." Jesus responded, "The ancients have written, 'A human being cannot exist on physical necessities alone but must also be sustained by spiritual resources.'"

---

ine the literary forms in which he cast his message. These scholarly pursuits have been undertaken by others, whose expertise in these matters exceeds our own.

We offer you a way of looking at the person of Jesus of Nazareth—his person, teaching, acts of healing, claims, final acts, and continuing presence. Alongside this exploration of Jesus, we listen to the testimonies of those who have met and known him. At the end of it all, we raise serious questions that everyone asks about him and suggest where persons in the twenty-first century may look for and meet Jesus Christ.

(continued)

The Adversary then set the stage for the second test. In a vision, he took Jesus up to a mountain and pointed to the various seats of power in the world. He said to him, "I have the authority to give all this power and the glory that goes with it to anyone I choose. If you will give your devotion to me, all of this will be yours." Jesus replied, "It is written, 'You must worship the Lord God and give your complete devotion to him.'"

For the third test, the Adversary took Jesus to Jerusalem and placed him on the uppermost part of the Jewish temple. Then he said to him, "If you are the Son of God, jump from this height. Surely you can trust the ancient record that says, 'God will send his special messengers to guard you and to catch you, lest you injure yourself.'" Jesus answered him, "It is also said, 'You must not force God to prove himself.'"

And when the Adversary had run out of tests, he left Jesus until a better time.

LUKE 4:1–13

DAY 8

JESUS' FIRST YEAR OF MINISTRY

Because some Jews were expecting the Messiah, some thought John the Baptizer might be he, so the leaders sent a group of religious officials from Jerusalem to make inquiry of John. They asked him, "Who are you?" Without a moment's hesitation John said, "I am not the Messiah." Then they asked him, "Are you Elijah, whom we have been expecting?" John answered, "No." "Are you that special spokesman who is to come?" Again John replied, "No." His interrogators persisted, "Who, then, are you? We must give an answer to those who sent us to interview you. What information can you

---

Jesus the Person

Jesus was born in a poor family; he grew up in a Jewish home that observed the Jewish laws and customs of the day. From his birth to the age of twelve, we know very little about him. It is likely that he learned to read, attended synagogue, and studied the book of Leviticus in the Old Testament, just as we would study a manual for right thinking and behavior.

(continued)

Suggestion #3
Think back over your early years. What were your first thoughts of God? Who taught you?

---

give us about your identity?" John said, "Go back and tell them that I am just a spokesman, declaring my message out here in the desert, saying, 'Prepare the way for the Lord,' just as Isaiah, the ancient spokesman for God, has said."

The persons interrogating John were a special group of pious rule keepers. Not being satisfied with John's answer, they persisted in questioning him: "Why are you administering baptism to people if you are not the Messiah or Elijah or that special spokesman of God who is to come?"

Again John responded, "I am indeed administering baptism with water, but there is another standing right here among us whom you have not recognized. He is the one whom I have described as succeeding me. He is actually greater in authority than I am. So great, in fact, that I feel unworthy to untie his shoe." This interview took place in Bethany, on the other side of the Jordan River in which John was baptizing the people.

On the day after that interview, John saw Jesus making his way to him. He said, "Look who is coming! He is the one who offers himself utterly to God, giving his life to put the whole world back on track. This is the man I have been talking to you about when I said, 'There is one coming who has authority over me because he has always been in existence.' For a long time I did not recognize who he was, but to prepare the way for his introduction to our nation, I have been out here baptizing persons with water. I saw the Spirit of God coming upon him and illuminating his whole being. It came like a dove from heaven. For a long time I did not recognize the special character of this person, but God, who commissioned me to baptize persons with water, said to me, 'Out of all those persons you will baptize with water, I will identify the one who is to baptize persons with the Spirit by permitting my Spirit to come upon him to fill and illuminate him.' And I

Jesus grew up in a rural culture in which most of the people were farmers. He learned from this environment about how farmers tilled small plots of ground and grew fruit, vegetables, corn, and wheat. He would have observed cattle and sheep and goats grazing on the hillsides. He knew how some of these animals were used in religious services for sacrifices, and knowing this may have been part of his thinking when he himself became a kind of sacrifice for the sake of the good.

He learned about the ways of God in a culture that was dominated

(continued)

---

want to go on record that I witnessed the Spirit of God coming upon this man as evidence that he is the Son of God."

JESUS TALKS WITH UNDERSTUDIES OF JOHN

The next day, John was talking with a couple of his understudies. He glanced up and saw Jesus again coming toward him and declared, "Take note of this person who gives himself so completely to God." Taking their cue from John, they went with Jesus. When Jesus noticed they were going with him, he asked, "What are you looking for?" They replied, "Teacher, where do you live?" He answered, "If you will come with me, I will show you."

They went with him and stayed with him the rest of the day, because it was then about four o'clock in the afternoon. One of these two men was Andrew, Simon Peter's brother. After his visit with Jesus, Andrew sought out his brother Simon and said, "We have discovered that specially anointed spokesman, 'the Christ.'" Then Andrew escorted his brother to Jesus. When Jesus perceived Simon Peter's inner being, he said, "You are now Simon, the son of John, but you will be named Peter, which means 'a rock.'"

The next day, Jesus went into Galilee where he met Philip, and he said to him, "Come with me and join my fellowship." Now, Philip's hometown was Bethsaida, the same as Andrew and Peter's. Philip sought out Nathanael and said to him, "We have talked with the person whom both Moses and the spokespersons of God foretold. His name is Jesus. He is from Nazareth, and his father is named Joseph." Nathanael was stunned. "Can anyone of worth come out of Nazareth?" Philip said, "Come and check it out for yourself."

---

by the Torah, the Jewish law. In his home, prayer was offered three times each day and weekly at commemorative meals; he and his family attended synagogue, where the Torah was read and prayers were offered. Three or four times each year, he and his family went down from Nazareth to Jerusalem to participate in the great festivals of the Jewish worship tradition. There was nothing somber or silent about these parades to the temple, where the faithful offered thanksgiving and songs of praise.

(continued)

When Jesus saw Nathanael approaching, he said, "Take note of this man. He is a true Israelite in whom there is no deceit." Surprised, Nathanael asked, "How do you know about me?" Jesus answered, "Before Philip invited you to meet me, when you were sitting in the shade of a fig tree, I saw you." Jesus' answer left Nathanael stunned. "Teacher, you must be the Son of God! You must be the king of Israel we have been expecting."

Jesus responded, "Do you say this just because I said that I saw you under the fig tree? If this incident overwhelms you, I tell you with certainty that greater things are about to happen. I tell you the truth," Jesus continued, "in the future you will see the sky open up and the special messengers of God traversing from heaven to earth through the Representative Man."

THE MIRACLE AT CANA

On the day after Jesus' encounter with Nathanael, there was a marriage celebration in Cana, a town in Galilee. Jesus' mother attended the wedding. Jesus and his understudies were also invited and attended. During the celebration, when the guests asked for more wine, Jesus' mother said to him, "They are out of wine." Jesus responded, "Mother, why are you giving me this information? That is not my responsibility or yours. Neither is it time for me to present myself to the people." Disregarding his statement, his mother said to the helpers standing by, "You do whatever he tells you to do."

By the entrance way were six large clay pots customarily used for religious rituals of purification. Each of them held about twenty or thirty gallons. Jesus said to the servants, "Fill each of these pots with water." They immediately filled each of them to the top. Then he said, "Now pour out a jarful and take it to the master of ceremonies." And they did as he had requested. When the master of ceremonies tasted the water, which had now

---

When Jesus was twelve years old, he attended one of these religious festivals in Jerusalem and stunned the teachers of the Torah with his insights and knowledge. Today, we would probably call such a person a religious genius. He amazed the teachers with his wisdom. After the festival, his parents began the walk back to Nazareth, and without knowing it for three days, they left him in Jerusalem. When they returned to Jerusalem looking for him, they found him talking with the religious leaders. On being questioned about staying behind, he told them, "Do

(continued)

become wine (he didn't know about the incident, but the servers did), he said to the man who was getting married, "You know, it's customary for people to serve their best wine first; then, when their guests have lost their sensitive taste, they serve cheaper wine. But you have reserved the best wine until now."

This is an account of the first miraculous sign that Jesus performed, in Cana, a town in Galilee. This is also the first instance in which he revealed his divine nature and his understudies trusted in him. After the celebration, Jesus went to his house in Capernaum, which was his headquarters. His mother, his brothers, and his understudies went with him, and they stayed together there for a number of days.

DAY 9

THE JEWS QUESTION JESUS' AUTHORITY

About that time, the nation was preparing to celebrate its deliverance from Egypt with the Passover. Jesus himself went up to Jerusalem to participate in the holiday celebration. On his arrival in Jerusalem, he went into God's house and found merchants selling oxen and sheep and doves. Others were sitting there changing money for the customers and charging high rates. When Jesus saw this, he made a whip out of small cords and used it to clear the temple of merchants, livestock, and the money changers. He said angrily to the merchants, "Take your goods and get out! How dare you make my Father's house a center of trade and commerce!" When his understudies saw what he did and heard what he said, they remembered one of the sayings: "Concern for the house of God will ultimately be my undoing."

you not know that I must be about my Father's business?" This statement indicates the first awareness that Jesus had of the meaning of his life.

After this bold act, the Jews asked Jesus, "What evidence can you present to prove you have the authority to do all this?" Jesus' answer was perplexing to them: "Get rid of this dwelling place of God, and in just three days it will be resurrected." The Jews mumbled among themselves, "Our ancestors spent forty-six years building this house of God, and you are to raze it, then resurrect it in three days?" They didn't know he was referring to his body as a dwelling place of God. After he was resurrected, his understudies remembered this encounter he had with the Jews and how he had promised the resurrection of his body. They trusted the record as well as what Jesus had spoken.

During the time that Jesus was in Jerusalem celebrating the exodus from Egypt, on the main feast day, many persons became his followers when they saw the miracles he did. But at this time, Jesus did not open himself completely to the people, because he knew what they would do. With respect to those who listened to him, he did not need anyone to tell him about them or about what particular people had done because he knew the motivation of every person.

WHAT THE SPIRIT DIMENSION IS LIKE

Nicodemus belonged to the party of pious rule keepers, and he also held a political office. One night he came to Jesus and said, "Teacher, all of us recognize that you are a true representative of God. All the miraculous deeds you have been doing convince us." Jesus did not respond to his affirmation but rather said, "I am telling you honestly that a person must go through an inner transformation, like being born a second time, before that person can have an awareness of the Spirit dimension."

Nicodemus responded, "How can this inner transformation, or this sec-

---

Jesus Is Tested

When he was about thirty years old, he went out to the desert along the Jordan River to be baptized by John, his cousin. John, who was six months his senior, told his audience that his task was to prepare the way for Jesus. By accepting John's baptism, Jesus identified himself and his interests with the poor, broken, marginalized persons of his day. Those were

(continued)

Suggestion #4

As you think back over the ways you have been tempted by appetites, pride, and the worship of false gods,

---

ond birth, take place when a person is an adult? Can he or she retreat into the mother's womb for another birth?"

"No," Jesus answered, "to enter the Spirit dimension, a person first must be born physically, then transformed spiritually. A person born physically is a human being; spiritual transformation opens one to the depth of being itself. With this explanation, you should not be amazed that I have said you must experience a second birth. The Spirit is somewhat like the wind blowing. You have seen the results of the wind blowing by the rustling of the leaves, but you do not comprehend its origin or its destination. In a sense, that's how the Spirit transforms your inner being."

"I really don't understand what you are talking about," Nicodemus insisted.

"You are a teacher in the nation of Israel, and you don't understand this?" Jesus asked. "I tell you the truth. I am describing a reality of which I'm certain; I am symbolizing for you what I have seen inwardly; and still I am not communicating with you. If I have endeavored to communicate with you with symbols from everyday life, what would it be like if I endeavored to communicate this spiritual reality with no images at all? No other human being has entered into the depth of being itself except the person who has come forth from the center of reality, even God's Representative Man, who at this moment still has his being in reality itself. Here's another way to symbolize my personhood: Moses put a snake on a pole out in the desert to heal people who were ill with snakebites; God's Representative Man must be put on a pole like that, so that whoever trusts in his person will receive healing and will be transformed to experience authentic life age after age.

"God loved the whole creation to the extent that the Holy One gave the Son, God's only Son, so that everyone who trusts him will not lose his life but will have authentic life age after age. God did not commission the Son to

the persons who submitted themselves to John's baptism.

what choices have you made?

Immediately after his baptism, Jesus went into the desert for a period of purification and testing. Why do you think that these tests come to persons on the heels of a high moment of achievement, self-realization, or divine recognition? The mountain-peak experience seems always to fall hard into the

(continued)

come into the world to condemn and negate human beings, but rather he came to liberate each of us so that we can have life. Everyone who trusts in God's Son is free from guilt and bondage. Anyone who does not trust in him remains guilty and in bondage because he does not trust God's one and only Son. This is the seriousness of bondage and guilt: the true purpose of life has appeared in the world, but humankind was more devoted to its own way of meaninglessness and despair than to life's true purpose, because they were controlled by evil. Those in the grip of evil despise the true purpose of life and don't expose themselves to it, because they would be compelled to change their lives. But the persons who are in harmony with reality do expose themselves to the true purpose of life, so that they demonstrate a life originating in God."

DAY 10

JOHN CLARIFIES HIS RELATIONSHIP TO JESUS

After this teaching episode, Jesus took his understudies into Judea, where he stayed for a while and baptized persons. About the same time John was baptizing in Aenon, which is near Salim. He had chosen that spot because there was a great deal of water there, and many persons were seeking his baptism. At this time, John had not yet been arrested and put in jail. Now, John's understudies got into a controversy with one of the Jewish leaders about observing religious rituals. In the midst of that controversy, John's understudies reported to him, "That man whom you baptized on the other side of the Jordan River, the one you witnessed about—we have reports that he is baptizing now, and most of the people are switching over to him."

John refused to be jealous or vie for prominence, saying, "No one can have any true authority unless it comes from God. You will recall that I told

---

valley of testing and temptation. Jesus' earliest followers believed that God sent him into the desert to face the kinds of temptations that come to all of us. His temptations ranged from yielding to physical passions, to succumbing to greed, to presuming on the power of God.

In the temptations that Jesus faced appear the primary tests of all human beings. Jesus, however, recognized the command "Turn these stones into bread" as a potential misuse of his power to satisfy his own physical appetite. Moreover, Jesus knew that bread alone did not satisfy the deepest longing of the human spirit.

(continued)

---

you very clearly, 'I am not the expected Messiah; I am simply his forerunner.' You know how it is at a wedding. The bride belongs to the bridegroom, but the best man, who listens to their vows, rejoices over what he hears them saying. And that's how I see myself in relation to the Christ. I have fulfilled my purpose. Now he must grow in his power and influence, while I must diminish in mine."

He comes out of the core of being, from which everything else has originated. A human being has ordinary origins and speaks as a mere mortal. But he is coming from the Spirit dimension and has priority over everything. The reality that he has seen and heard, he is communicating, but the people simply cannot receive his communication. Those persons who are able to hear his communication—by their acceptance—authenticate the presence of God in him. This person whom God has commissioned sets forth symbols and figures that come from God's own self, because there is no limit to the gift of the Spirit that God has given to him. God, our Father, loves the Son and has placed all creation under his control and management. Everyone who trusts in this Son of God experiences here and now the authentic life age after age, and everyone who closes him- or herself to a relationship with the Son does not experience life now or ever; rather, these experience rejection and alienation from God.

JOHN 1:19–3:36

DAY 11

THE WATER AND FOOD THAT SATISFY

About this time the pious rule keepers heard that Jesus attracted more followers and baptized more followers than John. (Actually, Jesus himself did

> At the same time, the temptation to jump thirty or forty feet from the temple pinnacle surely appealed to his pride. The suggestion from the enemy even had scripture to confirm it: "He will give his angels responsibility for you." Yet, Jesus did not depend on fate, heavenly beings, or social connections to make him feel important. He resisted what would have been a stunning act of power in the eyes of those witnessing it.
>
> Jesus never seriously considered the appeal to worship the devil; he refused obedience to anything that opposed the will of God. Even if the
>
> *(continued)*

not baptize anyone, but left that task to his understudies.) Jesus decided to leave Judea to avoid competition with John. On the way it was necessary for him to go through Samaria. During the trip, he traveled through the city of Sychar, which is located near the plot of ground that Israel's ancestor Jacob gave to his son Joseph. On that plot was located a deep well, known to everyone as Jacob's well. About noon, Jesus passed by the well and, being tired from the trip, he sat down by it. While he was sitting there, a local woman came to draw water. Politely, Jesus requested of her, "Give me a drink of water." (His understudies had gone into the city to buy food.)

The woman replied, "Aren't you a Jew? Surely you are aware that the Jews don't have any relationships with the Samaritans, and since I am a Samaritan, why are you asking me for a drink of water?"

Without acknowledging the racial implication of her question, Jesus simply said, "If you only understood what God wants to give you, and if you recognized who I am, you would say to me, 'Quench my thirst,' and I would quench your thirst for the meaning and purpose of life."

Thinking that Jesus was still talking about water in the well, the woman said, "But, sir, you don't have a line or a bucket with which to draw water, and this well is very deep. How would you quench my thirst? Are you superior to our father Jacob, who dug this well, who drank of it himself, and who shared it with his children and livestock?"

Jesus declared, "All who drink this water will need to drink again and again and again. But the person who drinks the water that I offer will never get thirsty, because the water I offer will be like an artesian well, springing up from a source deep within itself, continually quenching the thirst for the purpose and meaning of life."

With that, the woman said, "Sir, give me a drink of this water so that I

Adversary could have delivered the whole world to him, greed and lust for power were not the aims of his life. Whether first century or twenty-first century, these same temptations come to humankind: feeding the physical rather than the spiritual, displaying our powers to amaze others, and kneeling down to worship false gods.

Jesus successfully faced and dealt with every test given to him. After the period of testing, he began his ministry of teaching and healing. One of his first actions was to call "understudies" who were quite ordinary persons to join him. Many who joined him were from the ranks of the

(continued)

will never thirst again, and so that I will never come here to draw water again."

Jesus directed, "Go home and get your husband, then come back so we can continue our conversation."

The woman admitted, "I don't have a husband."

"That's right," agreed Jesus, "you don't. But you have had five husbands, and you are presently living with a man to whom you are not married, so you're right in saying you don't have a husband."

Shocked, the woman replied, "Sir, it appears to me that you are a spokesperson of God. Our ancestors worshiped God here on this mountain, but you Jews say that Jerusalem is the place where we ought to worship."

To this Jesus asserted, "Please believe me when I say that the place is not important; the time is coming when neither on this mountain nor in Jerusalem will people worship the Father. You Samaritans are not very clear about whom you are worshiping. In contrast, we Jews know whom we worship because liberation for all people comes through the Jews. The time is coming—in fact, it's here already—when genuine worship will arise out of a person's innermost being in accordance with reality, because that is how the Father wants to be worshiped. God is spirit, and authentic worship must be in accord with the worshiper's inner being, that is, in congruence with reality."

The woman stated, "I am aware that a Messiah is coming, one who will be called Christ. When he appears, he will talk about all God's purposes."

Jesus acknowledged, "I—the one speaking to you right now—am the Messiah about whom you have heard."

When Jesus' understudies arrived, they were shocked to find him talking

---

marginalized and powerless. His band of followers consisted of fishermen, tax collectors, zealous revolutionaries, and a host of no-names. The strength of his invitation gave them the courage to leave their secure lives, families, and vocations so that they might learn from Jesus and take part in his mission.

Jesus the Charismatic Leader

Jesus was without question a charismatic religious leader. By "charismatic" we mean that he was in contact with the invisible but real world.

(continued)

to the woman. Yet not one of them asked, "What are you trying to get from her?" or "Why are you talking to her?" Immediately the woman left the container in which she carried water, went into the city, and spoke to the people, saying, "Come meet a man who has revealed to me everything I've ever done. Is this the Christ?" They followed her out of the city to the well and approached Jesus.

While the woman was gone, Jesus' understudies said to him, "Teacher, eat your food." He replied, "I have food that nourishes me that you don't know about." This precipitated quite a discussion among the understudies, who asked, "Has someone given him food while we were gone?" Hearing them, Jesus said, "The food that nourishes me consists of living in accordance with the will of God, who commissioned me, and finishing the task God has given me. Hasn't one of you said recently, 'There are about four months until harvesttime'? Well, I ask you to open your eyes and look at the fields. They are already ripe for harvest. The person who harvests gets paid and, in addition to the temporal reward, receives authentic life age after age. The one who sowed the seeds originally and the one who participates in the harvesting share their joy together. The saying is really true: 'One person plants the seed and another reaps the harvest.' I am sending you out to reap a harvest where you did not plant seed. Other persons have prepared the ground, planted seed, and cultivated, and you participate in the benefit of their work."

A large number of the Samaritans who lived in that city believed in Jesus because of the woman's words "He revealed to me everything that I ever did." So when the people from the town got to the well, they asked him to stay awhile, so he remained there a couple of days. Then many more people trusted him because they heard him personally, and they said to the

---

He lived in harmony with the whole of reality, and not earthly reality alone. Like other charismatic leaders, Jesus believed in and had contact with the world of Spirit, the deeper dimension of existence. The religious tradition of which he was a part believed that in addition to the visible, material world there was a deeper world of spirit, not open to ordinary perception. This world of spirit was charged with energy and power; it embodied the holy or the divine.

For Jesus, this other level of reality was much more than a dimension of thought. It was a dimension of *experience*. He was actually drawn into

(continued)

woman, "We now have a relationship with him, not because of your report but because we have personally heard him. We are confident that he is truly the Christ, the liberator of the world."

After Jesus had stayed with them a couple of days, he went into Galilee. Already Jesus had stated, "A spokesperson for God is not recognized in his hometown." But then, when he came into Galilee, a number of Galileans related to him because they had personally seen what he did at the feast in Jerusalem.

JOHN 4:1–45

DAY 12

JESUS CALLS THREE UNDERSTUDIES

On one occasion, Jesus was standing by the lake of Gennesaret, and a large crowd gathered so close he was nearly trampled. He saw a couple of boats tied up by the shore. The fishermen had gotten out of them and were washing their nets. He got into Simon's boat and asked him to push out a few yards from the land. Then he sat down and began instructing the people. When he had finished teaching, he said to Simon, "Push out into deeper water and drop your nets for a good catch." Simon responded, "Teacher, we have fished all night and haven't caught a thing; but even so, I will do what you tell me." When they had pushed out as Jesus directed, the fishermen made such a good catch that their nets began to break. They called to their partners who were in another boat to come and help. They rowed over and filled both boats so full that they began to sink. When Simon Peter realized what he had witnessed, he got on his knees in front of Jesus and said, "Sir, I feel very uncomfortable in your presence because I am a crude and

---

this dimension, where he experienced the energy and power of the Spirit. Entering this level of reality resulted in a profound conviction about God and a power to teach, heal, and lead others to God.

At least three experiences during Jesus' lifetime illustrate his contact with the spiritual world. When he was baptized, he had a vision of the sky opening up and heard a voice speaking to him, "You are my son. I am pleased with you." Whether others heard this affirmation or not we do not know, but Jesus heard it.

Think of the amazing power that would come to a person to whom

(continued)

sinful person." Peter and those with him were awed at the large catch of fish. Simon's partners, James and John, Zebedee's sons, shared his awe. Then Jesus said, "Simon, don't be anxious. From this time on, you will gather persons together just as you have these fish." As soon as they docked their boats, they left everything to become understudies of Jesus.

LUKE 5:1–11

ISAIAH'S PROPHECY FULFILLED

Jesus had set up his headquarters in Capernaum, a seacoast town in the region of Zebulun and Naphtali. This choice fulfilled the prediction of Isaiah: "The region of Zebulun and Naphtali, which is by the sea, across the Jordan, next to Galilee, where live a number of non-Jews—the people who live in meaninglessness and despair have glimpsed reality, and those whose lives have bordered on death have tasted real life."

From that time, Jesus began his ministry, saying to all the people, "Change your attitude and actions because an invasion of the Spirit is imminent."

MATTHEW 4:13b–17

JESUS SHOCKS HIS AUDIENCE

Jesus and this small group entered Capernaum. On the Jewish day of worship, they went into the synagogue, and Jesus began teaching. The congregation was shocked by his boldness. He taught with his own authority, without quoting the rabbis, as the interpreters of the rules did. In this particular gathering there was a schizophrenic man, who interrupted Jesus in the midst of his lesson: "Let us alone, Jesus of Nazareth. Have you come to destroy our way of life? I recognize you as the special representative of God."

God says, "I am pleased with you." Is not this the ultimate affirmation that every human being longs for? Would this not confer on a person such a stable identity that the devil could not shake it? (Read the story on page 16.)

On another occasion, Jesus and three of his friends went up a mountain. While they were there, a thick cloud passed over them. They all heard the voice: "This is my much-loved Son, listen to him." This encounter with the beyond made a profound impression on the understudies of Jesus, but not deep enough to keep them from a tragic failure

(continued)

Jesus said to the separated part of this man, "Be at peace with yourself; let yourself be reunited." The man responded with groans, with tears, and with a loud shout; then he was reunited within himself. The whole congregation was amazed and excited. This incident provoked a flurry of questions: "What's going on here? What new teaching is this? With authority he speaks to persons divided within themselves, and they become whole persons." Immediately, Jesus' reputation spread throughout the countryside.

After this episode in the synagogue, the group went into Simon's house. Simon's mother-in-law had a fever, and they told Jesus. He came into her room, took her by the hand, and helped her out of bed. Suddenly her fever was gone, and she prepared food for them. After sundown, the entire community brought to Jesus their sick and distraught. It appeared that everyone in town gathered outside the house. Jesus healed many who were sick with different illnesses and made whole many distraught persons, while refusing to let them expose his true identity.

The next morning, he arose a good bit before daylight, went out to a solitary place, and prayed. When Simon and the others got up, they looked for him. When they found him, they reported, "Everyone is looking for you." Apparently oblivious to their statement, Jesus said, "Let us go on into the other towns and announce the good news about God's purpose to them, because that is why I am here." And he preached in all the places of worship throughout Galilee and made many persons whole.

MARK 1:21–39

JESUS FORGIVES SIN

After several days, when Jesus returned to Capernaum, word spread throughout the town that he was back. Right away, such a large crowd

---

later on. Even though it may not have sustained the followers, however, it supported Jesus in what lay before him in Jerusalem.

Jesus also seemed to be inspired by the Spirit when he said, "My Father, the source of everything that is in the universe, you have made it impossible for human strength to discover you, but you have revealed yourself to persons untutored in philosophy and ethics. . . . Father, you have placed everything in the universe under my authority. Among rationalists and moralists, not a person on earth knows who I really am;

(continued)

---

gathered at his house that there was no place even to stand. The crowd overflowed into the yard, and Jesus took the occasion to proclaim his message to them. While Jesus was speaking, a man stricken with paralysis was brought to the house by four friends. When they could not get the handicapped man through the crowd, they stripped the tiles from the roof and lowered him on his stretcher into the room where Jesus was standing. When Jesus recognized the faith of these four friends, he said to the paralyzed man, "Son, your sins are forgiven."

In the crowd were interpreters of the rules, who copy and study the Hebrew scriptures. They reacted negatively to Jesus' remark and thought to themselves, "Why does this man blaspheme? Only God can forgive sins." Jesus sensed what they were feeling and thinking. "Why do you entertain this attitude in your hearts? Which is easier to say to this sick man, 'Your sins are forgiven' or 'Get up, take your stretcher, and go'? So that you may be assured that the Representative Man has authority on earth to forgive sins, I will make this man whole." He said to the paralyzed man, "Get up, pick up your stretcher, and go home." At Jesus' instruction, the man got up, picked up his stretcher, and walked off in full view of everyone. The crowd was awed and extolled God's act in the healing. "Never before have we experienced anything like this!" they exclaimed.

JESUS ACCEPTS SOCIAL OUTCASTS

Jesus made his way to the seaside again, with the crowds following him. Again, he taught them. On one of his trips, Jesus passed the tax booth of Levi, the son of Alphaeus. Jesus said to him, "Follow me." And Levi followed him. He then invited Jesus to have dinner in his home; he also invited a number of his colleagues and people with bad reputations.

---

only you know me. But no person knows you either, except me and those to whom I reveal you." (See page 61.)

Can you imagine an ordinary man praying such a prayer? Jesus had such an openness to the other world that one could say he lived in the spiritual and natural worlds simultaneously. For this reason, he could communicate with his heavenly Father as confidently—or perhaps with even more confidence—than he could with his earthly father.

This experience of the spiritual dimension of being has long been a

(continued)

These social outcasts ate and drank with Jesus and his followers, and a number of them decided to associate with Jesus. But when the culturally elite interpreters of the rules and the pious rule keepers observed Jesus' practice of eating and drinking with these outcasts, they asked his followers, "How can your leader eat and drink with these social outcasts and violators of God's rules?" When his followers reported the query to Jesus, he responded, "Those persons who are whole do not need a doctor, but those who are sick. I have not come to change those who consider they are right but to enable those who are aware of their need to change their lives."

DAY 13

NEW WINE—NEW WINESKINS

Jesus had another encounter with the pious rule keepers. Several of them said to Jesus, "We fast. Even the followers of your friend John fast. But your followers are always eating and drinking. Why is this?" Jesus responded, "Can the friends of a groom fast on the eve of his wedding? While the groom is around, they don't even consider fasting. There will come a time when the groom is taken from them, and then they may choose to fast."

On another occasion, Jesus illustrated the effect of his mission on individual lives and social structures. "No person sews a piece of new cloth on an old piece of clothing, because when the new piece shrinks, the rip will be worse. No person puts new wine in old wineskins because when the new wine ferments, the skins will burst and both the wine and skins will be wasted. New wine requires new wineskins."

---

vital aspect of human reality. Only since the Enlightenment of the eighteenth century has this conviction about reality been pushed aside.

Marcus Borg, professor of religion at Oregon State University, speaks passionately to this point: "[The modern view] is historically the most recent and impressive because of the degree of control it has given us; but it is no more an absolute map of reality than any of the previous maps" (Borg, *Jesus, a New Vision,* p. 34).

The modern view of reality has given us another way of knowing.

(continued)

PEOPLE TAKE PRECEDENCE OVER RULES

Once, as Jesus walked through the grainfields on the Jewish sacred day, his followers pulled heads of grain and ate them, which was not considered lawful on that day. Again, the rule keepers queried him, "Why do your followers break the rules?" Jesus referred them to what one of their respected leaders had done: "Don't you recall what David and his associates did when they got hungry on the sacred day? Remember, when Abiathar was the high priest, how David went into the temple and ate the consecrated bread, which only the priests are permitted to eat? What's more, he gave some of the consecrated bread to his companions. The sacred day was set apart for human good, not the other way around. All the rules should be viewed in this way. Anyway, the Representative Man is the Lord of this sacred day, just as he is Lord of all the rules."

JESUS GETS RECOGNITION

On another sacred day, Jesus went into the Jewish house of worship. A man with a deformed hand was present. Jesus' critics observed carefully to see if he would cure the man, which also was against the rules, because they wanted this evidence against him. He asked the man with the deformed hand to stand up before the congregation. Jesus then addressed his critics: "Is it proper to do good on sacred days, or to do evil? Let me ask the question another way—is it right to preserve life, or to destroy it?" His critics remained silent, and he stared at them with anger and disgust because of their insensitivity to another human being's pain. Then he spoke to the man: "Stretch out your hand." As the man stretched it out, it became normal just like his other one. Then the pious rule keepers took the data they had gathered against Jesus and consorted with a political group who were loyal supporters of King Herod. Both these groups began to plot how they could get rid of Jesus.

But, while it has provided the foundation for science and technology, it has failed to give us a reason behind all the scientific discoveries and technological advances and thus has left many of us with an emptiness that we cannot fill.

Borg candidly states, "The world-view that rejects or ignores the world of Spirit is not only relative, but is itself in the process of being rejected. The alternative to a one-dimensional understanding

(continued)

Suggestion #5
Have you ever looked at a mountain and wondered, "Why?" Did you ever have an experience that gave you

---

While they were scheming, Jesus withdrew to the seaside. Numerous persons from Galilee and Judea followed him. A huge crowd gathered from Jerusalem, Idumea, the region beyond Jordan, and from Tyre and Sidon, because they had heard of the astounding healings that had taken place. Some came out of curiosity, while others came seeking wholeness in their lives. Jesus requested that his understudies prepare a small boat for him, so he could avoid being pressured by the crowd. Because he had made numerous persons whole, many in the crowd, hoping to be healed, pressed against Jesus just to touch him. Quite often persons who were in deep emotional distress tumbled on the ground before him, screaming, "You are the Son of God." But Jesus was quick to tell them to keep his identity secret.

MARK 2:1–3:12

The mighty acts that Jesus continued to perform fulfilled the prediction made by Isaiah, the spokesman of old. He had said, "Observe my chosen representative, the one whom I love very dearly, the one with whom I am delighted. I have placed my spirit in him, and he will reveal the right thing to the non-Jews. He will not fight, neither will he complain. No person will witness him crying in the streets. He will not add to the oppression of anyone; neither will he intensify the suffering which they experience until the way that he represents prevails throughout the earth. And because of him, the non-Jews will have hope."

MATTHEW 12:17–21

JESUS CHOOSES HIS INTIMATE UNDERSTUDIES

About this time, Jesus withdrew to a mountain to pray, and he prayed to God all night long. After a night of prayer, he beckoned his understudies and chose twelve of them to be ones he would send out to share in his

---

of reality can claim most of the history of human experience in its support" (p. 34).

People through the centuries in different cultures have regularly experienced the dimension of the Spirit. Perhaps Jesus opens the way for "moderns" to recover an awareness of and a participation in this dimension of reality that has been squeezed out of our consciousness by one-dimensional thinking.

pause? Did God ever seem like more than a word to you?

mission. He chose Simon, whom he also nicknamed Peter; Simon's brother Andrew; James and John; Philip and Bartholomew; Matthew and Thomas; James whose father was Alphaeus; and Simon, who was a revolutionary. He also chose Judas, James' brother, and Judas Iscariot, who later betrayed him.

LUKE 6:12–16

After Jesus selected these twelve and stated what he wanted from them, they went back down the mountain to his house. The crowd gathered again, making it virtually impossible for them to eat. When Jesus' friends and family heard about his activities, thinking that he was beside himself, they sought to take him back home. His brothers and his mother came to the place he was teaching and called out to him. When Jesus did not respond, someone in the crowd yelled, "Your mother and your brothers and sisters are calling you." Jesus asked, "Whom do you consider to be my closest relatives?" Then, as he looked from face to face, he answered his own question: "You are my closest relatives. Whoever fulfills the intention of God, that person is like a brother or sister or mother to me."

MARK 3:19b–21, 31–35

DAY 14

ATTAINING FULFILLMENT

On these occasions, when large crowds gathered, Jesus would make his way up a mountain, and his understudies would join him. Here is a summary of the things he taught:

"O, how fulfilled are those who recognize their own poverty of spirit, because they shall enter the Spirit dimension.

Jesus the Teacher

The records indicate that Jesus, in the midst of a complex social and political environment, spent much of his time teaching persons about their relationship with God. His teachings were couched in Jewish-style wisdom sayings, stories, and parables.

Many of the wisdom sayings of Jesus are found in what is referred to as the Sermon on the Mount. Before his day, the wise men of Israel had thought long and hard about the ways of God. They had struggled with

(continued)

"O, how fulfilled are those who let themselves feel the full intensity of their pain, because they will ultimately experience complete joy.

"O, how fulfilled are those who have all their instincts under control, because they will be in harmony with all of nature.

"O, how fulfilled are those who hunger for right relations in all things, because they will find them.

"O, how fulfilled are those who can forgive other people, because God will forgive them.

"O, how fulfilled are those who know who they are and what they are to do, because they will experience God in the depths of their being.

"O, how fulfilled are those who create unity and harmony between others, because they will be identified as God's offspring.

"O, how fulfilled are those who endure pain and persecution for their part in the God movement because they will enter the Spirit dimension.

"Each of you will be fulfilled despite the verbal incriminations or physical attacks made against you. Celebrate your participation in the God movement now and the participation you have in the final triumph, which also is yours.

"You are the seasoning of the world, but if the seasoning loses its taste, it is good for nothing but to be cast into the garbage.

"You are a flashing light in the flow of history, showing it the way. A large beacon that is set on a hill cannot be hidden. No person lights a lamp and covers it with a black cloth, but rather one holds it in one's hand so that it can shine on the pathway for others to see the way. Let your own actions light the way of other persons so that they may discover the way to live and, knowing that the source of your being is in God, they will fulfill the divine purpose and plan with gratitude.

---

the demands of the law of God and the hard realities of their lives. In this struggle, they had come to insights into the true ways of God and had often condensed their wisdom into short, pithy statements. Some of Jesus' statements seem to take up the same task of teaching the way of God in condensed sayings. For example:

"O, how fulfilled are those who recognize their own poverty of spirit, because they shall enter the Spirit dimension."

"O, how fulfilled are those who let themselves feel the full intensity of their pain, because they will ultimately experience complete joy."

(continued)

JESUS POINTS BEYOND THE LAW

"Do not interpret my ministry and message as wiping out your law or the words from long ago. I have not come to destroy the past but rather to fulfill that which was always present in it. I tell you the truth, until the ultimate consummation of history, not one part of your past, not a word or even a letter, will be abolished until it comes to pass.

"If any, therefore, try to abolish these rules, and if they teach others to do the same, they will have only a minor place in the Spirit dimension; but those who recognize their true intent and share their insight with others, these persons shall participate fully. I tell you this, though, unless your relationships flow from the heart and not from the head, as do those of the interpreters of the rules and the pious rule keepers, you will not participate in the Spirit dimension.

"In the past, your teachers have said, 'You shall not kill, and offenders who do kill will have to face the consequences of their action.' But I tell you, those who are unjustifiably angry with another person will have to face the consequences of their feelings. If persons call others bad names, they will have to give an account of this behavior in court. And those who discount other persons will be in danger of losing their own personhood.

"So if you are ever praying or offering your gifts to God in worship and recall one of your fellow human beings who has a case against you—drop your praying; stop your worship; go find your brother or sister and make peace; then come and offer your prayer and your worship. Develop the habit of agreeing with persons who antagonize and oppose you when it does not cost you your integrity. To foster arguments will result in lawsuits, courtroom scenes, and even jail. Such is costly to both person and purse.

"O, how fulfilled are those who have all their instincts under control, because they will be in harmony with all of nature."

"O, how fulfilled are those who hunger for right relations in all things, because they will find them."

"O, how fulfilled are those who can forgive other people, because God will forgive them."

"O, how fulfilled are those who endure pain and persecution for their part in the God movement, because they will enter the Spirit dimension."

In that same collection of sayings, Jesus offered shocking directions.

(continued)

"Your teachers years ago said, 'Do not commit adultery.' I tell you that adultery is more than an act; all who mentally picture having sex with a person have already committed adultery in their inner beings.

"Let me make some comparisons between physical values and spiritual values. If your right eye sees things in such a way that it blocks your spiritual growth, pull your eye out of its socket and throw it away, for it is more desirable that one member of your body be lost than that you lose the whole purpose and meaning of your life. Or, if your right hand behaves so as to block your spiritual growth, cut your hand off and throw it away, for it is more desirable that you lose one of your members than the purpose and meaning of your life.

"You also recall that your teachers of old said, 'If anyone wearies of living with his wife, all he need do is formally dismiss her, and that absolves him of all responsibility for her future welfare.' I say to you, whoever dismisses his wife without evidence that the relationship is already broken and dead causes her to commit adultery. Whoever marries one who is so divorced also commits adultery.

"Your teachers of old have also said, 'Do not swear falsely, but perform to the Lord what you have sworn to do.' I say to you, don't swear at all. Don't swear in heaven's name, for that really refers to God. Don't swear by the power and meaning of the earth, for that is God's, too. Don't swear by holy places, for they, too, belong to God. Don't swear by your own integrity because you can't change your essential being. You are persons of integrity. Say simply yes or no. To amplify your statement by swearing in the name of heaven, of God, of the earth, of a holy place, or yourself reveals your ignorance of yourself.

"Your teachers a long time ago said, 'Avenge evil; take an eye in place of

---

"Love your enemies; affirm those who discount you; be kind to those who fear you; and ask God to enlighten the manipulators and the profiteers. I ask you to live like this so that you reflect the mind and spirit of God, who makes the sun light the paths of both the perverse and the straight and brings rain on everyone's land, whether they worship him or not." (See full text on page 40.)

Another of Jesus' teaching methods focused on parables. A parable is a short story with a hidden point. When you first read a parable, the meaning seems obvious. But then it awakens a question, and you begin

(continued)

---

an eye, or a tooth in place of a tooth, if yours is destroyed.' But I tell you, don't fight back. If a person slaps you on your right cheek, present the left cheek also. If someone files a suit against you and would take away your coat, give that person your overcoat as well. And if a stranger asks you to walk one mile, be willing to walk two. Give assistance to the person who asks for your help. For example, if a person seeks a loan, try to accommodate that person.

"The teachers of old said, 'Love your neighbor and hate your enemy.' I say to you, love your enemies, affirm those who discount you, be kind to those who fear you, and ask God to enlighten the manipulators and the profiteers. I ask you to live in this manner so that you may be a reflection of the mind and spirit of God, who makes the sun light the paths of both the perverse and the obedient and causes it to rain on everyone's land, whether the person worships the Lord or not.

"What value is it if you love those persons who love you and are kind to those persons who are kind to you? Even evil persons can return kindness for kindness. If you recognize and honor only those with whom you are intimate, what is the difference between you and other people? Do not even those who have no awareness of God do that? My final admonition to you is to be as fully human as God is fully God.

INWARD MOTIVATION VERSUS OUTWARD ACTS

"Now, let me talk with you about the inwardness of a person's relation to God. Regarding your contributions to worthwhile causes: do not stage your giving so that you will get attention from others, because if you do, you may escape your heavenly Father's attention. When you make your contribution, don't hire musicians to get the world's attention, as the great religious

---

to wonder. A parable has enormous power to undermine how people look at the world and how we interpret our experiences.

Jesus often used these "stories with a point" to communicate the values associated with the Spirit dimension—the nature of the spiritual world and how persons enter into it. For example, he told parables about persons who would sell everything they owned to possess a field with a certain treasure in it; about a farmer sowing seed in different kinds of soils with different results. He taught the amazing power of faith to move mountains and to endure temptation.

(continued)

pretenders do. When they get the world's applause, that is all they can expect from their giving. When you give to worthy causes, keep your action a secret even from yourself; don't tell your neighbor, and don't keep replaying your act of charity in your head. Keep your anonymity. You may be sure that your heavenly Father is aware of your generosity and will fulfill you with the gift of the divine Spirit.

"Like giving, prayer is also a personal experience. When you offer your prayer, don't seek a place of public display, such as places of worship, athletic contests, political gatherings, or the speeches of public officials. Those who pray there have their recognition from the crowds who hear them. When you pray, withdraw into your inner being, where you are alone with God. As your prayers flow from there, your life will clearly demonstrate you have been with God.

"Also, when you offer prayers, don't be wordy like the uninstructed. Prayer is more than words; it is attitude, awareness, and action. Thus, a lot of words do not mean a lot of prayer. I emphasize to you that God is aware of you before you are aware of God, and God knows what you need before you utter a single word.

DAY 15

GOD SEEKS YOUR INNER SELF

"Here is a simple way for you to pray: 'Father, you are the heart of heaven. We reverence your name. May the movement of your being continue to its ultimate fulfillment. May your purpose be actualized on this earth. May it be demonstrated in our lives as completely as it is in heaven. Enable us to receive the physical necessities for our lives today. Continually forgive our

---

Jesus was a great storyteller. He spoke of a man who had two sons; one took his inheritance and wasted it, while the other stayed at home working for the father. He told about a woman who lost one coin and searched for it until she found it. He spoke of a lender giving money to people, requesting them to manage it and return to him a profit. He described a landowner who left his property under the care of a manager, only to return and find that the manager had been unfaithful to his charge. These stories served to call into question the world as his audi-

(continued)

---

failures, even as we forgive the failures of others. Lead us by your hand. Do not test us. Liberate us from destructive structures and persons. I pray all of these things because yours is the power, the authority, and the fulfillment in all things, in all ways.'

"When you understand and accept other persons' failures, it is not nearly so difficult for you to believe that your Father understands and accepts you. If you cannot understand and accept other persons' failures, how can you believe that your Father will understand and accept you?

"Let me now point out to you the spiritual meaning of abstaining from food. When you decide to abstain from food for a period of time, do not act like the great religious pretenders, who neither wash their faces nor comb their hair. They march about with a sad expression on their faces so that it will be obvious to other people that they are abstaining from food. Truly, I tell you, they have all the fulfillment they will get.

"When, for spiritual reasons, you decide to abstain from food, then wash your face and comb your hair so that your friends and acquaintances will be unaware of your decision. But during these times, present yourself to your Father in the inner depths of your being. There your Father will see your true motivation and will reveal the divine presence in your life.

FULFILLMENT FOUND IN THE SPIRIT DIMENSION

"Do not seek your security in the accumulation of possessions. The treasures of this world are subject to corruption and decay; if their values increase sufficiently, someone will find a way to take them away from you. I do suggest that you accumulate wealth for yourself in the spiritual dimension of life. In that dimension, there is no corruption or decay; nor is there

---

ence perceived it. The stories also provided instruction for living in the Spirit dimension.

One of Jesus' stories has been told and retold thousands of times. For some reason, it seems to capture most of us with its sudden turn and strange ending. This is the well-known story of the son who asked his father for his inheritance before his father died, a deed tantamount to saying, "I wish you were dead." The father strangely complied with his request and gave him his part of the inheritance.

The young son took the inheritance, left home, and went abroad. He

(continued)

deceit and deprivation. Whatever you place the highest value on, you will propel your life in that direction.

"Remember how your eye sees for your body. If your eye is in focus, then your body will have good, clear direction. But if your eye is diseased and out of focus, your vision will be impaired, and you will lose your sense of direction. Now, if the inner light of your being goes out, you will be in the dark concerning the meaning and direction of your life—and how great will that darkness be!

"No person can live with dual loyalties. That would be self-destructive schizophrenia. When persons find themselves in a conflicting situation, they must choose one and reject the other; they must devote themselves to one to the neglect of the other. You simply cannot live with a double loyalty—one to God and the other to material things.

"When you have asked your Father to help you obtain the physical necessities of life, do not be filled with anxiety about what you will eat or drink or wear. Remember, life is more than food and clothes. Also, take note of the birds flying in the sky; they do not sow seed, reap harvests, or store grain, and yet your Father sees to their needs.

"Compare yourself with birds. If you should wish to change the gifts of nature with which you have been endowed, just how much do you suppose you could change your being? Consider the anxiety that you often feel about the clothes you have. Just look at the flowers growing in the garden. They spring up and grow and bloom. They don't work at growing and making themselves beautiful. Didn't I tell you that our wealthiest king, Solomon, was not clothed as elegantly as one of those blooming flowers in your garden? If God wishes to color the world with beautiful flowers, which

---

found numerous new friends as long as the money lasted, and he experienced life as never before—hard drinking, drugs, and plenty of sex.

The money ran out; the friends did, too. And, as they say in Alcoholics Anonymous, he hit bottom. Looking around and finding himself to be a bum on the street, he suddenly felt hungry, with no money for food. Just for a few crumbs, he began washing dishes at the "greasy spoon" café. Bending over the sink, staring at dirty pots and pans, he came to himself. "My dad's housekeeper fares better than this!"

He decided to go home and face his embarrassment and the punish-
(continued)

are here today and gone tomorrow, do you not think God will put clothes on you?

"Again, I repeat, do not live with anxiety; don't keep asking, 'What shall we eat? What shall we drink? Where will we get our clothes?' This continuous quest for more and more of the physical necessities occupies the full attention of those who are unaware of God's presence. I assure you that your Father, the source of your being, is aware of all your physical needs.

"You are to give first priority to the Spirit dimension and to setting all your relationships right. When you get a proper perspective, these other things will take care of themselves. So I tell you, live in the here and now. Don't worry at all about tomorrow. Live tomorrow when it gets here; deal with its challenges and opportunities as they present themselves.

DON'T EVALUATE OTHER PEOPLE

"Do not spend your time deciding whether people are good or bad, and then you will not fear that they or God are deciding whether you are good or bad. Whatever standard you use to evaluate other persons, you will use the same standard to evaluate yourself. And with whatever limited knowledge you measure out their punishment, you will measure out your own.

"In the process of evaluating another person, why do you see a speck in a brother's eye while you are oblivious to the log in your own? I must say, it is quite presumptuous for you to offer to wipe a speck out of his eye when you may jab his good eye with the log in your own. O pretender, take the log out of your eye so that you will not injure your brother when you are wiping the speck out of his. Maybe when you suffer the pain of removing the log, you will become more sensitive to speck wiping.

"Do not expose the deepest values and motives of your life to persons

---

ment of his dad. All the way home, he rehearsed his story: how bad he had been, how he didn't deserve anything, and . . .

When he got near home, his dad saw him coming and ran to meet him. (In Jesus' culture, mature men never ran, especially to meet such an embarrassing failure!) The son began his confession: "I have . . ." But before he could force his confession through his lips, his dad called members of his household staff and told them to dress the boy, to put a ring on his finger signifying that all was forgiven, and to prepare a banquet.

(continued)

who cannot appreciate them, and don't talk with them about things that are most meaningful to you. Such vulnerability will probably permit them to cause you pain and suffering.

DAY 16

GUIDELINES FOR YOUR LIFE

"Here are three simple directives for living in the Spirit dimension: ask for what you want, and you will get it; seek for what you need, and you will find it; knock on doors, and they will open to you. I repeat: all who ask for what they want get it, and all who seek for what they need find it, and all who knock on the door find it opened. Fathers, listen to me. If your son should ask you for a piece of bread, would you give him a rock? Or if he should ask you for a piece of meat, would you give him a live snake? If you, then, being human, respond to the legitimate desires and needs of your children, will not your heavenly Father, the source of all things, give you the true needs of your life?

"Live by this axiom: whatever you would like for yourself, grant that to every other person. When you treat others with this love, trust, and respect, you fulfill everything that the rules laid out and that the ancient spokespersons of God talked about. Choose God's way and give it priority in your life, because there are many easy choices you can make that will lead to meaninglessness and despair, and many persons will choose those routes. Because the choice to express the Spirit dimension requires you to focus your life and bring it under control, few people will choose it. They would rather keep all their options open, a course that results in the loss of life and meaning.

With this son home again, the father and his friends began to celebrate in a way you wouldn't believe. (See the rest of the story on pages 107–8.)

Anyone reading this story can get the thrust of its meaning. Most of us can find the runaway son inside ourselves, along with his failure; we can find the stay-at-home son inside us, too. (You have to read the rest of the story to find out about the son who stayed home.) In both cases, we are confronted with a parent who loves despite the failure of the two boys. Hardly anyone can seriously read this story without yearning for

(continued)

"Look out for pious religious pretenders who appear to be sensitive and sincere but inwardly are motivated by greed and the lust for power. You will recognize the source of their motivation by their behavior. You know that you don't gather grapes from blackberry vines, nor figs from cactus. It takes a strong, healthy tree to produce good, edible fruit. And a blighted tree produces shriveled fruit. A healthy tree will not produce blighted fruit, nor will a blighted tree produce edible fruit. When you have a tree that does not produce good fruit, you cut it down and burn it up. I have given you these illustrations about trees and fruit to illustrate that behavior reveals the nature of a person's heart.

BELIEF INCOMPLETE WITHOUT CONGRUENT BEHAVIOR

"While I am speaking about behavior and motivation, let me say that not every person who says the religious words 'Lord, Lord' will enter the Spirit dimension; rather, it is the person whose behavior is congruent with God's intention who will enter the Spirit dimension. On the day of the ultimate fulfillment of history, many participants in the building of that history will say the religious words 'Lord, Lord,' and they will even say, 'We have preached; we have healed schizophrenia and other mental disorders; we have done many good things.' But I will have to say to them, 'Regardless of your words and your benevolent actions, you never really participated in the Spirit dimension. Get away from me. You have actually done evil rather than good.'

"With this presentation I have summarized my teaching about the Spirit dimension. If you can hear what I am saying to you and shape your life according to the principles I have laid down, you will be like a wise person who built his house on a firm foundation. And all the elements in nature tried to destroy that house: it rained; it flooded; the winds blew; the

---

an encounter with the waiting father. But when you know the cultural norms, you recognize that the father contradicts all the expectations of his friends and fellow citizens in how he deals with both sons.

In this story and others like it, Jesus turned on its head the established world of his hearers. So when you read his stories, whether this one or others, expect them to contradict much in how you see the world and how things are.

At the core of Jesus' teaching were stories and parables about the deeper dimension of life, the Spirit dimension, that sometimes are called

(continued)

trees fell. But the house stood firm because it had a solid foundation. And those of you who are hearing the sound of my words but making no decision about your behavior will be like a foolish person who erected his house on sand. When the rain and wind and floods came, that house collapsed, and its destruction was a tragedy."

When Jesus had outlined these principles to the crowd, they were astonished. They found it difficult to accept his teaching. And yet, he instructed the people as one having his own authority, not like the interpreters of the rules, who depended on the authority of others.

JESUS HEALS

When Jesus had concluded his teaching, he came down the mountain accompanied by large crowds. On the way to his headquarters, he was met by a leper who bowed to him in reverence and said with great faith, "Sir, if you choose, you can make me whole." Contrary to common practice, Jesus touched the leper saying, "I want you to become whole." At once, the leprosy disappeared. Looking deeply into the man's eyes, Jesus instructed him, "Do not tell a single person what I have done; rather, present yourself to the religious leaders and make the kind of contribution that is prescribed in the rules. Let both your gift and your presence witness to them."

As he entered Capernaum, a Roman army officer came to him with an urgent request: "Sir, I have a servant at my house who is paralyzed, and he is suffering beyond description." "Then I will come and make him whole," replied Jesus. Anxiously, the soldier spoke up again: "Sir, even with my station and rank, I don't deserve your coming to my house, but if you will just say the word, I believe that my servant will be made whole. You see, like yourself, I am a man with authority. I have soldiers under me, and I say to

---

"kingdom parables." He taught about how God wanted life on earth to be; he called this "living in the Spirit dimension." Sometimes he spoke of this dimension as present and breaking into human history. After his baptism, he came into Galilee saying, "The time has been fulfilled, the presence of God is at hand, repent and believe the good news."

Jesus told a story to illustrate how this presence spreads. This Spirit dimension, according to Jesus, is like seed cast on soil. Some seeds are cast on hard, packed soil and never take root. Other seeds are cast on soil that has no depth, and they wither in the heat. Still other seeds are

(continued)

this one, 'Go!' and he goes, and to another one, 'Come!' and he comes, and to a servant in my household, 'Do this!' and he does it."

The official's response so amazed Jesus that he turned to the crowd following him and said, "I tell you the truth, I have not experienced this depth of faith before, not even in the chosen people who presumably have faith. Because these chosen people do not demonstrate genuine faith, there will come a time when other persons will be gathered together from the East and the West, and they will have fellowship in the Spirit dimension with Abraham, Isaac, and Jacob. But those who originally were destined for the Spirit dimension will be left with no purpose and direction, and the pain of their existence will be unbearable."

After issuing this brief rebuke to the chosen people, Jesus turned to the soldier and said, "Go on home. Because you have believed the truth, your request is granted." From the time Jesus made that declaration, the official's servant was healed.

MATTHEW 5:1–8:13

Although Jesus endeavored to keep a low profile, his reputation spread everywhere. And great crowds gathered to hear what he had to say and to receive his touch of healing. Because the pressure of the crowds drained him, he often secluded himself in the desert to pray.

LUKE 5:15–16

DAY 17

THE FARMER AND HIS SEED

On another occasion when Jesus was by the sea, he again began teaching his followers. Because they were so numerous, he got into a small boat and

---

cast on soil with weeds, and after sprouting, they are choked out by the weeds. A few seeds fall on well-cultivated earth and bring forth an abundant crop.

In this story about the seeds, Jesus illustrates the different modes of consciousness that we bring to his teaching. The seed story suggests that some persons never hear or take his teaching seriously. Others listen for a time but then become distracted. Others listen and obey, but then competing loyalties choke their good resolve. Finally, some hear and obey the message, and their lives reproduce the Spirit of Christ.

---

sat there while the crowd stood along the shoreline. He presented his message in stories to help them see his meanings. In one of his presentations he said, "Listen to this. A farmer began planting. In the course of his planting, some of the seed fell on the hard path, and birds swooped down and ate these. Some of the seed fell on a thin layer of soil with a thick rock ledge underneath. These sprouted quickly and came up immediately, because they were planted near the surface. But when the sun came up, these plants withered because they had no depth. Some seed fell in the midst of thorns. The thorns grew with the good seed, choking the vitality out of the plants so that they never bore fruit. Yet other seed fell on good soil. These sprouted, produced strong plants, and reproduced—some thirty, some sixty, and some a hundred times as much as the initial planting." Jesus concluded, "If you can understand this story, appropriate its meaning for your life."

After the crowd dispersed, he was left with the Twelve and a few others who were attracted by his story, which carried a spiritual meaning, and they asked him for an interpretation. He explained, "You who share this mission with me are to understand the mystery of the Spirit dimension, but those who are not participating with us receive only the stories. Those outsiders see the picture, but they don't grasp its meaning; they hear the words, but they don't understand their significance. If they did experience the meaning of the stories, their lives would be transformed and their misguided actions forgiven." Then he said, "If you do not understand this story, how can you understand my other stories?

"Here's the explanation. The planter plants an authentic witness of God in every relationship. Planting on the hard earth is like an encounter with God that is superficial, because it does not penetrate that person's defenses.

The Spirit Dimension

In another story about the other dimension, Jesus spoke of a person finding "the pearl of great price." When he found this pearl, he sold everything that he possessed in order to purchase it. Jesus' point was that life in the Spirit dimension is of more value than anything or everything that we possess. Perhaps he also meant that to live in God's presence costs us everything.

(continued)

Suggestion #6

Read the parable about the soils on pages 48–50 and try to identify which type of consciousness you have.

Immediately the Adversary snatches away the memory of the meeting. Those persons represented by the thin layer of earth are those who immediately celebrate an encounter with God. But the joy is short-lived because they do not open their inner being to the Spirit, and soon the surface encounter withers. The seeds sown among thorns are like persons of wealth or power who are distracted by other interests that quickly consume their experience of God. The seeds sown on good ground are like those encounters with God in which an authentic relationship is established. These seeds sink in, grow, and bear fruit—some thirty, some sixty, and some a hundred times as much as the initial planting."

MARK 4:1–20

JESUS DESCRIBES THE SPIRIT DIMENSION

Jesus continued, "The Spirit dimension is like a seed planted in the earth. A person plants it, then sleeps and rises night and day. The seed sprouts and grows, though the planter doesn't understand how. The earth has power to reproduce naturally—first the blade, then the stalk, and finally the full wheat. When the wheat matures, the planter gathers it in, because the harvest is ready.

"Again, how shall I describe to you this Spirit dimension? To what can I compare it? It is like a single mustard seed, which is one of the smallest seeds sown on earth. After it is sown, it grows into the largest of shrubs. Its branches shoot out in such size that birds come to rest in its shadow."

Using symbolic stories like these, Jesus taught his followers about the Spirit dimension, careful always to give them no more than they could handle. He always spoke to the crowds in stories, refusing to give them expla-

---

As part of the Spirit dimension, Jesus taught about forgiveness, forgiving, and being forgiven. On one occasion, a member of his little community said, "How many times should I forgive my brother when he does something wrong to me? Seven times?"

Jesus responded, "Seventy times seven." He meant forgiveness without limit. Jesus taught that we should live a life of compassion. To make the point, he told the story about a man who was trav-

(continued)

Which would you like to have?

nations. But when he was alone with his understudies, he explained the special meaning of his stories.

A FURTHER REVELATION OF POWER

One evening, after teaching the better part of the day, Jesus said to his followers, "Let's go over to the other side of the sea." They dismissed the crowd and pushed off from the shore, with Jesus in the boat. There were several small boats near them. Suddenly a storm arose, and the waves tossed the boat about, filling it with water. During the storm, Jesus was asleep in the stern. The understudies woke him, shouting, "Teacher, don't you care that we are in danger of drowning?" Jesus arose and spoke with authority to the wind and the sea, saying, "Settle down; be at peace." Immediately, the wind stopped blowing and the sea quit churning, and a deep stillness came. Then he spoke to his followers: "Why are you so frightened? Where is your trust?" Afraid and perplexed, they questioned one another: "Who is this person that even the wind and the sea respond to his directions?"

DAY 18

JESUS REUNITES A FRAGMENTED PERSONALITY

They crossed the sea and landed in the region of the Gerasenes. When Jesus got out of the boat, he was immediately accosted by a demented man who was living in the cavelike tombs common in the area. He came dashing up to Jesus—he was so fierce that no person had been able to control him, not even with chains. Those living around him had repeatedly tied him with chains and shackles, but each time he got loose. Nothing could

---

eling from Jerusalem to Jericho. On the way he was attacked by bandits. They beat him and took everything he had.

After a time, two religious people, a priest and his assistant, passed by, and on seeing the plight of the man they passed him, getting as far away as possible. Then a Samaritan (a person hated by the Jews and considered to be an outcast) came along and helped the man who had been beaten and robbed. He even took the man to an inn and paid his bill.

In this story, Jesus in a subtle way rebuked the snobbish Jewish leaders

(continued)

---

restrain him. Night and day he was in the mountains or inside the caves, screaming and cutting himself with stones.

When this tortured man saw Jesus at a distance, he ran to him and worshiped him. Then he cried out to Jesus, "How am I related to you, Jesus, Son of the Most High God? In the name of God, please don't torture me anymore." Jesus responded, "Come out of this man, alien destructive spirit." Then he said to the separated parts of the man, "What is your name?" The parts answered, "'Many'—because my personality is split into many parts." The estranged parts of the man begged, "Do not banish us from this country. If we must go, let us enter the pigs feeding on the hillside." When Jesus directed these fragments to leave, they entered the pigs, making them dash headlong down a steep slope into the sea, where they drowned. (There were about two thousand of them.)

The men who tended the pigs fled into the city and told what they had seen. People from the city and surrounding countryside went out to witness the incident for themselves. They first came to Jesus; then they saw the demented man quietly sitting beside Jesus, fully clothed and mentally together. They were frightened. The witnesses related what they had seen happening to the man who had been separated from himself and what had happened to the pigs. The crowd began urging Jesus to leave their community. Jesus responded by getting into the boat. The man who had been made whole pleaded with Jesus to let him accompany Jesus. Jesus refused: "Go back home to your friends and tell them what God has done for you and how God has cared for you." The healed man left and traveled throughout the region of the ten cities, telling his remarkable story of what Jesus had done for him. His hearers were awestruck.

---

of his day and pointed to the way of compassion as the way to live in the Spirit dimension.

Again, Jesus taught the way of love. A lawyer asked him, "Teacher, among all the rules we have been given, which do you consider superior?" Without any hesitation Jesus answered, "'You are to love the Lord your God with all your feelings, with all your inner being, and with all your intelligence.' This is the number-one rule, and the second rule is quite similar: 'You will love every person just as you love yourself.'"

By the commandment to love, Jesus did not mean that we are to have

(continued)

REMARKABLE FAITH

Jesus got into the boat and returned to the other side of the sea. A crowd was gathered right up to the water's edge, and out of the crowd stepped a man named Jairus, an official from the local synagogue. When he got to Jesus, he fell at Jesus' feet and pleaded, "My daughter is ill at home, and I fear she is dying. Please come with me and lay your hands on her body and heal her, so she will live." Jesus responded to his request and went with him, the crowd following closely behind.

In the crowd was a woman who had had a menstrual problem for twelve years. Though she had already been treated by many doctors in the region and had spent her last cent, she grew no better but rather worsened. The woman had heard of Jesus' healing ministry, so she made her way through the crowd and touched his clothes. She said to herself, "If I can touch his clothes, I will become whole." Indeed, when she touched him, her bleeding stopped immediately, and she knew in herself that she was healed. When Jesus sensed that healing power had gone out of him, he turned to the crowd and asked, "Who touched me?" His understudies replied, "You see this crowd milling around you—it could have been a dozen persons. How can you ask such a question?"

Jesus studied the faces in the crowd to see who had made contact with him. The woman knew what had happened to her, and she was frightened as Jesus looked at person after person in the crowd. She anxiously stepped forward and fell down before him, confessing what had happened. Gently, Jesus said to her, "Your trust has made you whole, daughter. Go your way in peace, and continue to be well."

While he was talking with her, messengers from the official's house

---

warm, fuzzy feelings about everyone all the time; rather, we are to show goodwill, make allowances, and desire the good of all. What a simple and powerful vision for a complex world!

---

arrived and said to Jairus, "Your daughter is dead. Don't bother the teacher any longer." When Jesus heard the report, he said to Jairus, "Do not panic. Only trust."

For the remainder of the trip he permitted only Peter, James, and John to accompany him. When they came to Jairus's house, they found confusion, with everyone crying and grieving the child's death. On entering the house Jesus asked, "What is going on here? Why the uproar? This child is not dead. She is merely asleep." Their mourning suddenly turned to scorn when the mourners felt themselves under attack. When Jesus had dismissed them, he took the father and mother with his companions into the room where the child was. He then took the little girl by the hand and said, "Little girl, get up." Immediately, she sat up and walked around. (She was twelve years old.) All who witnessed it were awed. Jesus insisted that no one was to know about the incident. "Give the girl some thing to eat," he added.

MARK 4:26–5:43

BLIND AND MUTE MEN HEALED

When Jesus left the house of the Jewish official and started back to his headquarters, he noticed two blind men calling aloud to him, "David's son, help us! Help us!" They followed him all the way to his home, even into the house. Jesus said to them, "Do you believe that I can cause you to see?" "Oh, yes!" they declared. He then touched their eyes with the tips of his fingers, saying, "What you have believed in the depths of your being will be true in your body." Their eyes were healed, and they could see again. Immediately, Jesus clearly instructed them, "Don't tell anyone what I have done. I don't want anyone to know about it." Quite contrary to Jesus' request, they left

---

Jesus the Healer

Jesus was more than a Jewish charismatic prophet who went about the countryside teaching people about an incursion of the Spirit dimension. Jesus also healed people of various illnesses.

A leper came to him saying, "If you want to, you can make me whole." Jesus responded, "Of course I want to," and he reached out and touched him and immedi-

(continued)

Suggestion #7

As you read the things Jesus taught about living in this other dimension of reality, try to imagine

---

his house and told their experience to everyone they met. Jesus' reputation spread throughout the countryside.

As soon as these two men left, a man was brought to him who was unable to utter a single word. He had not always been that way but had had an experience that left him speechless. When Jesus removed his speech impediment, the man immediately began to talk. The crowd again was gripped with amazement, saying, "Our nation has never seen such before." But the rule keepers, quite unwilling to believe that God was acting in this man Jesus, said, "He gets rid of these infirmities with power from the ruler of destruction."

MATTHEW 9:27–34

DAY 19

JESUS' SECOND YEAR OF MINISTRY

Jesus went to Nazareth, where he had been reared. As he had been brought up to do, he went to the place of worship on the sacred day. On entering, he requested the scroll and asked permission to read. They gave him the scroll of God's spokesperson Isaiah. Jesus unrolled it and found the place with this special message: "God's Spirit has come upon me because he has given me a special commission to proclaim the good news to poor persons. He has sent me to proclaim liberation to the enslaved, to give vision to the blind, to free the oppressed, to announce this is the time of God's action." Then Jesus rolled up the scroll, gave it back to the attendant, and sat down. Everyone present focused attention on him when he said, "Today this forecast has come to pass in your presence." And everyone who encountered

ately the leprosy disappeared. This healing incident has a number of amazing points. Jesus actually touched this leper, an act forbidden by Jewish law. He cured him. He sent the leper on his way with the instruction that the leper tell nobody about the experience.

Jesus met a man in the synagogue (a place of worship for the Jews). The man shouted, "I know you. I know who you are. You are the holy one of God." Jesus spoke to the separated part of this man and

the world he envisioned.

(continued)

him was pleased at the encouraging words he spoke. They asked, "Isn't this Joseph's son?"

Anticipating their response, he remarked, "You will probably quote one of our sayings to me, 'Doctor, make yourself well. Whatever you've done in Capernaum, do here in your hometown.'" Then he remarked, "Honestly, no spokesperson for God is listened to by his own people. Let me remind you that there were many Israelite widows in the time of Elijah's ministry. You will remember that it didn't rain for three and one-half years, and hunger was rampant throughout the land. I remind you that Elijah didn't go to any of the widows in Israel but to Zarephath, a city of Sidon, to a Gentile widow. At the time of Elisha, another of God's spokespersons, there were many lepers in our nation. He did not heal any of them, but rather he healed Naaman the Syrian."

When Jesus implied that God gave preference to Gentiles, he really made the Jews angry. They were so furious that they carried him out of town to the crest of a hill to throw him off a steep slope. But somehow, he walked right through them and got away.

LUKE 4:16–30

COMMISSIONED FOR MISSION

After teaching in the villages a while, he brought together his twelve understudies. Dividing them into pairs, he commissioned them to share his ministry and gave them authority over the forces that destroy persons. He gave them instructions for their travels: "Do not take life's necessities with you. Take only a walking stick, no bag, no bread, no money. Wear shoes and take only one coat."

He continued, "When you enter a community, settle in a home that wel-

---

commanded that alien part of him to leave. In his day, they called this "casting out demons." This man was also made well. (See pages 30–31.)

One of Jesus' followers was named Peter. His mother-in-law had a fever. On entering her house, Jesus was informed of her illness. He placed his hand on her, and the fever departed.

On another occasion, Jesus was at home in the small village of Capernaum. Hearing that he had returned from his teaching mission, the whole village gathered at Jesus' house. Four men carried a paralyzed friend to the house, and when they could not get the paralytic in the door,

(continued)

---

comes you and stay with them until you leave. Do not be discouraged by those who do not respond to your message. When you leave, shed your feeling of responsibility and wipe the dust of remembrance off your shoes. You have given them my word; their response is their responsibility. On the final day of reckoning those persons will have no excuse."

MARK 6:6b–11

"Let me forewarn you about some of the experiences you will encounter on your journey. I am asking you to be as nonresistant to evil as sheep are to vicious wolves. Be as wily as a snake and as innocent as a dove. Be wary of your listeners. Hidden in the crowds will be persons who desire to take you to court, and others who will beat you even in religious meeting houses. During your mission, you can expect to be brought before the governing authorities because of the witness you are making on my behalf.

"When you are apprehended and dragged into court, don't worry in advance about what you will say. When it is necessary for you to bear witness, you will receive sudden inspiration at that very moment concerning what you are to say. Be confident that when you speak, it is not some tale you have contrived, but the Spirit of God who speaks through you.

"Not only will vicious men try to destroy you, but because of your message, whole families will be divided: brothers will oppose brothers, parents will oppose their children, and children will oppose their parents, even causing them to be executed. And persons from all walks of life, from all the communities you visit, will despise you because you preach my message and participate in my mission. But the person who perseveres to the end of time will find personal wholeness and fulfillment.

"When the resistance becomes too great in one city, go to another. You

they tore off the roof and lowered him into Jesus' presence. Jesus spoke to the paralyzed man, "My son, your sins are forgiven." After forgiving the man, he told him, "Get up. Pick up your mat and go home." The town folk were amazed.

We do not know how Jesus made these persons whole. Perhaps he was in touch with the Spirit dimension so fully that its power and energy flowed through him. Maybe God acted through the words

(continued)

Suggestion #8
Read the story of the healing of the paralyzed person (pp. 31–32). Identify with one of the persons at Jesus'

will not have covered all the cities in this nation before the Representative Man makes his appearance. Expect that.

"Keep in mind that the student is not above the teacher, nor the employee above the employer. It is enough to expect the student will become like the teacher and the employee like the employer. Now, consider a specific application of that insight. If our opponents have called the head of the house 'the prince of devils,' what do you suppose they will say about his children? Regardless of what they say, don't be afraid. One day the truth will be known by all, and at that time your true motives, as well as those of your opponents, will be exposed for everyone to see. What I have shared with you in the long nights of training, proclaim courageously in broad, open daylight. What I have whispered in your ear, shout on the street corners of the city.

"Again I say to you, don't be afraid of those who can destroy your body but have no power to touch your spirit. Rather, reverence the one who is the source of both your spirit and your body. Stay in touch with your source. You are aware that you can buy a couple of sparrows for a penny. Don't you know not one of those can fall wounded to the earth without your Father being aware of it? God knows everything about you, even how many hairs you have on your head. Do not be anxious for your safety, because persons are much more valuable than sparrows. Remember that whoever speaks my name and my message before other persons, I will confess his name and his faithfulness before my Father who is in heaven. Conversely, whoever denies my message before other persons I will repudiate before my Father who is in heaven."

MATTHEW 10:16–33

"I have come to start a process of judgment, and it appears to me that some wish it had already started. I myself have an ordeal to experience, and

---

and the touch of Jesus of Nazareth to heal people and to show signs of the Spirit dimension erupting into human history.

We cannot explain these miracles of healing. They are attested by his followers. Yet, Jesus did not measure his ministry by miracles. What we call miracles were responses of compassion to human suffering and need. Consider Jesus, the one who came into our history to make persons whole.

house and relive the story as that person. When everyone has left, you are left alone with Jesus. Ask him your deepest

(continued)

I am already feeling the pressure until it is over with. Do you think that at this time I am going to unify all persons and groups on earth? I am telling you that I will not, but rather, I will cause division. For example, there will be five people in a family, and they will be divided three and two against each other. A father will be opposed to his son and the son opposed to his father. The mother will be opposed by her daughter and her daughter will be opposed by her mother. The mother-in-law and daughter-in-law will be in opposition to each other.

LUKE 12:49–53

"But remember that a person who loves father or mother more than me cannot have a genuine relationship with me. And a parent who loves son or daughter more than me cannot have a complete relationship with me. Anyone who does not take his commitment to me with utmost seriousness, even to giving his life for me, cannot have a mature relationship with me. The person who experiences a full relationship with me will discover real life, and his unproductive relations will fall away. The person who loses these old relationships because he is related to me will certainly find real life.

"Because you are related to me, everyone who relates to you relates to me, and everyone who relates to me relates to the one who sent me. The person who respects the spokesperson of God and relates to that person as such will participate in that spokesperson's reward. In like manner, the person who appreciates the value of another person's relationship and respects him for his lifestyle will participate in the benefits of it. Let me apply these simple principles to the task you are undertaking. Whoever recognizes you and gives you a drink of water because you are my understudy will relate to me through you."

After Jesus' departure from the earth, his followers continued to gather in his name. When they gathered, they often told the stories about Jesus that they remembered. When they told these stories, two things often happened: they were drawn into an encounter with his living presence, and they were made whole. In addition to showing the compassion of Jesus, these stories still, after two thousand years, have the power to draw us into the Spirit dimension and to mediate healing and a sense of his presence with us today.

question, and listen for his answer.

DAY 20

ABOUT JOHN THE BAPTIZER

After Jesus had concluded his instructions to his twelve understudies, he left the headquarters to join them in teaching and preaching in nearby cities. When John the Baptizer, who now was in jail, heard reports of the marvelous activities of Jesus, he felt the need for personal reassurance. So he sent two of his own understudies to Jesus with this question: "Are you the person we have expected to come all through the ages, or must we still wait and look for him?" Rather than give a direct yes or no answer, Jesus said to John's followers, "Report to John once again the things that you yourselves have heard and seen, namely, blind persons are seeing; lame persons are walking; leprous persons are made whole; deaf persons are hearing; dead persons are coming to life; and poor persons are hearing good news that liberates them. Remind John that every person will be fulfilled who does not give up trust in me."

When John's followers were out of earshot, Jesus turned to the crowd and spoke about John the Baptizer: "When you went out into the desert to hear what the Baptizer had to say, what did you expect? Did you expect a man who had bent to popular opinion, as a reed responds to a stiff wind? What did you expect? Did you expect to find a man dressed in stylish clothes? Those stylish dressers are among the elite. Again I ask, what did you expect to see in the desert? A person who would tell things as they are? Well, that is exactly what you found, and even more than that. For the spokesman you went to hear is the one written about in our ancient scriptures: 'Take note, because I send my representative before you to prepare the way for you to walk in.' I tell you the truth, there has never been a person born who is greater than John the Baptizer. Still, the person who is born into the Spirit dimension has a greater awareness and perception than he does. From the time John the Baptizer began his ministry, the Spirit dimension has been under attack, and those persons bound to rules and regulations have sought to force their way into it. You see, until John made his appearance, the spokespersons of old and the lawgivers had spoken of the future. If you can believe it, the Baptizer is really Elijah, whom you have expected to return and initiate a new era. If you have ears, then listen to what I am saying.

"I have searched for a symbol that would best express your actions and responses. You are like children sitting on the curb of the road yelling out to your playmates, 'We have made music, but you won't dance with us; we have cried our eyes out, and you won't shed a tear.' You see, John presented himself as an ascetic, and you said, 'He is possessed by an alien spirit.' The Representative Man came as a regular person, eating and drinking with the people, and you say, 'Look at that glutton, that wino; he is a bosom buddy of tax collectors and disreputable people.' Oh well, I suppose that true wisdom can never be found in what a person does and doesn't do, if that's all the information you have about him."

WORDS OF WARNING AND COMFORT

Jesus pointed out to the people that not only were they rejecting his own life of social engagement; they were also rejecting John's ascetic way of life. Jesus went on to reprimand those from the nearby cities, because they had witnessed the actions of both John and Jesus and had changed neither their attitudes nor their actions.

"Beware, Chorazin! Beware, Bethsaida! If the ancient cities of Tyre and Sidon had witnessed the deeds that you have witnessed, their change of attitude would by now have been reflected in the transformation of their lives. Remember this: in the day of final reckoning, things will go easier for Tyre and Sidon than for you! A special word to you, Capernaum, in whose bosom I have made my headquarters. You have been exalted to the heights, but you will be brought down to the depths, for daily you have witnessed the power of God acting through me. If the evil city of Sodom had seen these deeds, it would have remained until this very day. Likewise, on the day of final reckoning, it will go easier for Sodom than for you!"

When Jesus had spoken these words, he seemed to be transformed by the Spirit, and he uttered this prayer: "My Father, the source of everything that is in the universe, you have made it impossible for the rationalists and the moralists in their own strength to discover you, but you have revealed yourself to persons untutored in philosophy and ethics. Yes, Father, this was your way of showing people that they are dependent on you. Father, you have placed everything in the universe under my authority, and not a person on this earth knows me for who I really am; only you know me. But no person knows you either, except I and those to whom I reveal your nature."

When he had concluded his prayer, he reached out his arms to the crowd around him and said, "Come into fellowship with me if you are tired and burdened, and I will refresh and release you. Take the burden of responsibility I give you and thereby discover your life and your destiny. I am gentle and humble. I am willing to relate to you and to permit you to learn at your own rate. Then, in fellowship with me, you will discover the meaning of your life. Fellowship with me will release you, and my companionship will direct you on your journey."

MATTHEW 10:37–11:30

THE DEATH OF JOHN THE BAPTIZER

It was about this time that Herod, the governor of the region, began hearing reports about the phenomenal activities of Jesus. Out of his sense of guilt, he said to several of his associates, "This man is John the Baptizer. He has come back to life, and that's why these miraculous healings are taking place through him." Herod had arrested John and put him in jail at the insistence of Herodias, his wife, who had been married to his brother Philip. On one occasion John had said to Herod, "It's wrong for you to be living with her." He would have killed John at that moment, but he was afraid of the crowds, since they considered John to be a spokesman for God. When, however, Herod celebrated his birthday, Herodias's daughter performed an erotic dance. Greatly stimulated, and without thinking, Herod offered her anything she wanted. Directed by her mother, she said, "Present me with John the Baptizer's head on a platter." Her request grieved Herod, but he was faithful to his word and directed that her request be granted. At his instructions, the soldiers beheaded John, who was in jail. Then his head was placed on a platter and given to the young woman, and she took it to her mother. John's associates claimed his body and buried it, then went to tell Jesus what had happened.

MATTHEW 14:1–12

DAY 21

JESUS FEEDS THE CROWD
SPIRITUAL AND PHYSICAL FOOD

About this time, the twelve understudies with whom Jesus had chosen to share his work returned from their trip. They reported to him what they had been doing and teaching. Because they were exhausted, he invited them into a deserted place to relax. This withdrawal was made necessary by the crowd of persons who had come to Jesus that he might minister to them; there had been so many people that the understudies had had little time even to eat. They embarked in a boat to a place of solitude. When the people saw Jesus leaving, they anticipated where he would go and met him there.

When Jesus got out of the boat, he saw that a sizable crowd had gathered, and he was moved deeply by their needs. He perceived them as children without parents, and he began to care for them with such earnestness that all were oblivious to time. Finally, his understudies interrupted him: "It's getting late, and there is no food here. Dismiss this crowd so they can find food for themselves in the village or from friendly folk in the countryside." Jesus said, "You give them something to eat." The understudies responded, "Do you want us to spend all the money we have for food and give it to them?" He asked, "How many loaves of bread did you bring for us?" They checked and reported: "Five loaves and two fish." Jesus told the crowd to sit down on the grass, and they clustered in groups of fifty and one hundred. Picking up the five loaves and two fish, Jesus looked up into the sky and blessed the food, then broke the loaves and gave them to his understudies to offer to the crowd. Likewise, he divided the fish among them all, and all present ate until they were satisfied. After the meal, the understudies filled twelve baskets with leftover bread and fish. About five thousand ate the loaves and the fish that day.

JESUS AGAIN SHOWS MASTERY OVER NATURAL LAWS

At once, Jesus instructed his understudies to get back into the boat and return to Bethsaida while he dismissed the other people. Sending them home, he went up the mountain to commune with God. Late in the evening, the boat with his understudies was in the middle of the sea, and Jesus was alone on the mountain. From his position, Jesus could see the boat. In the early morning, he saw his understudies struggling with the oars because the wind was against them. He walked out on the sea and came close to the boat. He would have passed them by, but they saw him and mistook him for a spirit.

Shuddering, they shrieked in deep distress. He at once spoke calmly to them: "Take heart, it is I; don't be anxious." As he walked over to the boat, the wind ceased. The understudies were filled with immeasurable wonder and amazement. Awe pervaded their minds. They had been unable to appropriate the meaning of the loaves and fish because their spiritual perception was dull.

Jesus and his understudies went across the sea and landed in Gennesaret. As soon as they stepped out of the boat, the people recognized Jesus. Wherever Jesus went, the people brought their sick to him. When they could not converse with him, they lined the road hoping just to be able to touch him. Those who did were healed.

MARK 6:30–56

Jesus went out of that area into the region of Tyre and, desiring solitude, entered another house. He wanted to conceal himself from the people, but he could not. A woman with a sick child found his hiding place and thrust herself into his presence, falling at his feet. The woman was a Syrophoenician by birth, and she asked him to make her mentally ill daughter whole. Jesus responded to her: "A man must first satisfy the needs of his family. It is not customary to take food from the family and give it to strangers or foreigners." The woman agreed. "But," she added, "strangers are given the leftovers from the family table." Jesus said to her, "Because of your response of faith, the illness that tormented your daughter is gone." When this mother returned home, she found her daughter recovered and resting in bed.

JESUS RESTORES HEARING AND SPEECH

Jesus moved on from Tyre by way of Sidon to the Sea of Galilee, through the region of the ten cities. On his journey, a person was brought to him who was deaf and could not speak clearly. Those who had brought this man requested that Jesus touch him and make him whole. Jesus took the fellow's hand and led him away from the crowd. Placing his fingers in the man's ears, he spat and touched the man's tongue. Jesus lifted his eyes toward the sky and sighed deeply, "Be opened, ears." That very moment the fellow's ears were sensitized and his tongue relaxed, so that he heard and spoke clearly. Jesus urged the man and his friends to keep the healing a secret, but the more he urged, the more they publicized his healings. Those who both experienced and witnessed his healings were astonished beyond description: "He makes everyone whole. He even causes deaf persons to hear and mutes to speak."

DAY 22

ANOTHER MIRACULOUS FEEDING

During these days of Jesus' ministry, the crowds that collected around him were huge. On one occasion, he called his understudies out of the crowd and spoke these words to them: "I feel a deep concern for this crowd because for the three days they have been listening to and traveling with me, they have had nothing to eat. If I send them home without food, I fear they will pass out along the road, because many have come a great distance." His understudies responded, "How can you or anyone else provide food out here in this desert?" "How many loaves of bread do you have?" Jesus asked. "Seven," they responded. "Sit down on the ground," he instructed the crowd. And he took the seven loaves, offered thanks, broke them, and gave the bread to his understudies, who distributed it to the people. He did likewise with a few small fish that his understudies had found. The crowd ate its fill, and together they took up seven baskets of leftovers. The crowd numbered about four thousand. After he dismissed them, Jesus entered a boat and went to Dalmanutha.

MARK 7:24–8:10.

While there, the rule keepers and the religious aristocrats sent delegations to interview Jesus. They demanded, "Give us indisputable evidence of your identity and what you are up to." In response Jesus said, "Late in the afternoon you survey the sky. If it appears to be red, you predict fair weather for the next day. But when the sky is dark and threatening, you predict rain. You pretenders! You can read the message written in the sky, but you cannot read the meaning of the events that are happening right around you. You are a blind and confused generation with divided loyalties, and no convincing evidence will be given to you except Jonah's sign of hope." Jesus turned around and walked away from them. He and his followers got into a boat and sailed back across the sea. When they got to the other side, they remembered that they had taken no food. Jesus turned to his followers, saying, "Take note of the yeast of these pious rule keepers and proud aristocrats." His followers began to speak among themselves, "What's he talking about? Yeast? His symbols confuse us. He must be referring to the fact that we didn't bring any bread along."

When Jesus realized what they were talking about, he said, "You have so little trust in me, and what I can do! Don't you remember the day we fed five thousand persons with five loaves of bread? How many sacks of leftovers did you pick up that day? Don't you remember the seven loaves of bread with which we fed four thousand people? How many sacks of leftovers did you pick up that day? Surely you understand that I am not talking about bread and your failure to bring some along! I am speaking to you about the influential teaching of those two groups of leaders—those who are pious legalists and those who are skeptical aristocratic rulers." The followers got the point. They realized he was not talking about bread at all but about the influence that the ideas of the rule keepers and religious aristocrats could have on them.

MATTHEW 16:1–12

DAY 23

A HEALING ON THE SACRED DAY

A little later, the Jews had a celebration in Jerusalem, which Jesus attended. Now, in Jerusalem there is a pool next to the Sheep Gate that is called

Bethzatha. It has five porches around it. On these porches would gather a large number of sick persons—blind, crippled, and paralyzed. The sick would lie on the porches waiting for the pool to bubble up, because whoever steps into the pool first after it bubbles will get well. One of the persons lying there was a man who had been ill for thirty-eight years. When Jesus saw him and realized how long he had been sick, he asked, "Do you want to get well?" The sick man replied, "Well, yes, but I don't have anyone to put me into the pool when it bubbles up. While I am struggling to get in, someone beats me to it." With a ring of authority Jesus said, "Get up, pick up your mat, and go." Suddenly, the man realized he was well. He picked up his mat and went home. All this took place on the Jewish sacred day.

The man who was cured was accosted by Jews who said, "It is our sacred day! You are breaking the law by carrying your mat." The man answered, "The person who made me whole said to me, 'Pick up your mat and go!'" So they asked him, "Who is this fellow who told you to pick it up and walk?" The man who was made whole was embarrassed because he didn't know the answer.

In the meantime, Jesus had slipped through the large crowd that had gathered. Later, Jesus met this man in God's house and said, "Indeed, you are well. Avoid those practices and attitudes that are destructive to you, lest you suffer worse consequences."

After this instruction, the man departed and told the Jews, "Jesus is the one who made me well." As soon as they heard this, these Jews began to plot against Jesus, because he had done these things on the sacred day.

When confronted, Jesus said, "My very own Father has been working up until this time, and I myself have been working with him." At that statement, these Jews became more infuriated than ever and sought to kill Jesus, not only because he had violated the sacred day but also because he had claimed that God was his own Father, asserting that he was divine. Jesus dealt with them by saying, "I speak the truth to you when I say that I do not concoct my lifestyle, but I discern how my Father is acting and I join him in his activity in the world. My Father loves me and enables me to discern what he is doing in the world. Later on, he will enable me to discern even more than I do at present, and you will certainly be amazed at that. My Father is able to raise persons from death and give them life, and he has given me the authority to give life to whomever I will. He does not judge persons but has given me the authority to make all evaluations. All persons should reverence me just as they do my Father. Anyone who does not reverence me does not reverence my Father who has sent me.

"I tell you the truth regarding everyone who hears what I'm saying and trusts the one who has sent me—these persons have authentic life age after age and will never be condemned, because they have been transformed out of death into life. Listen when I say, there will come a time, an hour, when those who lie in death will hear the voice of God's Son. Everyone who hears will live. The Father who is the source of life is not dependent on anyone else to give him life. In like fashion, the Son is a source of life for himself and others. God has also delegated authority to the Son, the Representative Man, to pronounce the final judgment of persons.

"Don't be shocked at what I am saying. There is coming a time that everyone who has sunk into death will hear God's voice. Everyone will experience resurrection: resurrection to life for those who have done good, and resurrection to death for those who have done evil. I don't do all these things by myself. Whatever I hear from the Father influences how I make decisions, and my decisions are fair because I do not seek to do what I wish but what the Father wishes. The Holy One has sent me and works through me. If what I am saying to you is mere fantasy, then it's not true at all.

"Yet, there is another one who attests to what I'm saying. I know that his evaluation of me is accurate. You Jews sent a delegation to John the Baptizer, and he told you the truth. Yet I really do not need the attestation of a man, but I point to this evidence so that you may find a right relationship with God. John was a brilliant witness reflecting God's light into your lives, and for a time you celebrated the witness he was giving.

"Though I have pointed you to John, I have stronger evidence than his witness regarding the task that my Father has delegated to me: the way in which I perform this task and the result of my performance attest that my Father has commissioned me. And furthermore, even the Father who has commissioned me has certified me. None of you has ever heard God speak, nor have you seen the shape of the Holy One. God does not control your lives, as evidenced by the fact that you do not believe in me.

"You are daily searching your records and laws. You think that knowing these rules will give you authentic life age after age, but your records merely forecast my coming to you. And still you decline to enter into a relationship with me so that you may find life. I do not look to other persons for the source of my recognition and approval. I recognize that the source of your life is not the love of God. I have presented myself to you as a representative of my Father, and you have not responded to me. If another person comes on his own behalf, you will attach yourself to him. How impossible it is for you to trust what I am saying while you are seeking recognition and approval from one another and not from God alone! Don't worry about my accusing you to the Father. The rules that you trust will accuse you sufficiently. If you had really understood those rules that Moses gave, you would have responded positively to me, because he wrote about me. If you don't trust what he wrote, how can you trust what I say?"

JOHN 5:1–47

Even after confrontations like this, a pious rule keeper invited Jesus to dinner. He accepted and went to the man's home. In that particular city was a woman who had a bad reputation, and when she was aware that Jesus was eating in the pious man's home, she brought a bottle filled with perfume. For a while she stood behind Jesus; then she knelt down and wept and washed his feet with her tears. Wiping his feet with her hair, she kissed them and poured the perfume on them. When the pious man observed what was taking place, he said sarcastically, "If this man were a spokesman for God, he would know who this woman is and what kind of life she is living. He would recognize what her feeling and touching him means, because she is a disreputable person." Jesus responded, "Simon, I have something to tell you." "Go ahead, teacher," the rule keeper countered, "tell me."

"There was a lender who had loaned two people money," Jesus told him. "One of them owed five hundred dollars, and the other owed fifty. When they couldn't pay, he canceled both their debts. Tell me, which of them will be most appreciative?" Simon responded, "I suppose the one who had the larger debt canceled." "Right," Jesus said. Then Jesus turned and looked at the woman as he spoke to Simon. "Just look at what this woman has done. I came to your house, and you didn't rinse my feet as gracious hosts do, but this woman has bathed my feet with tears and dried them with her hair. You didn't greet me with an embrace and a kiss on the cheek, but from the time I got here, this woman has not stopped kissing my feet. You didn't bother to greet me with any warm gestures, but this woman has poured expensive perfume on my feet. So I want you to know that all of her past is forgiven and wiped out, and she is filled with love because of it. But you realize that the person who is forgiven only a little experiences only a little love." Then Jesus said to the woman, "Your past is forgiven." When the guests who had been invited to the dinner party heard that remark, they whispered among themselves, "Who is this man who forgives sins?" Then Jesus spoke to the woman, "Your trust has made you whole. Go out and be the person you truly are."

LUKE 7:36–50

DAY 24

JESUS JOURNEYS WITH HIS COMPANIONS

The next day Jesus and his understudies, accompanied by a crowd, went to Nain. On the outskirts of town, he met a funeral procession. The dead man was the only son of his mother, who was a widow, and most of the people in town were in the procession. When Jesus saw this woman, he felt deep compassion and love for her and said, "Don't grieve." He then went over and touched the casket, and those who carried it stopped. He said, "Get up," and the fellow sat up in the casket and began talking. Jesus helped him out and sent him home with his mother. Those who observed this miracle were filled with awe and offered their thanks and praise to God. They said, "He is a remarkable spokesperson for God. God himself has visited us." The report of this incident spread throughout all of Judea and even the neighboring regions.

LUKE 7:11–17

In the course of his ministry, Jesus, always accompanied by his twelve understudies, went into cities, towns, and villages proclaiming and demonstrating the good news of the Spirit dimension. Also with him were several women who had been liberated from emotional and physical illnesses: Mary Magdalene, who had been cured of a severe case of personality disorder; Joanna, the wife of Chuza, who was an employee of Herod the tetrarch; and Susanna. Also in the group were other women who looked after everyone's needs through their giving.

LUKE 8:1–3

On one occasion, a person was brought to Jesus who was deeply divided within himself; he was also blind and speechless. Jesus united this man to his true self and enabled him to see and speak. A sense of awe swept over the crowd when they saw what he did. They said, "Isn't this the son of David, the new king whom we have been expecting to deliver and rule us?"

GOD IS NOT DIVIDED

The mention of a new ruler threatened the rule keepers, and they made their attack: "This man has been given all this power by the ruler of the demonic." When Jesus heard their pronouncement, he said, "Every nation that is divided against itself will be destroyed, and every city or household divided against itself will fall down. And if the ruler of the demonic dimension attacks the demonic, then the ruler of all evil is divided against himself. How can the demonic dimension stand if it is divided? If I make people whole by the power of the demonic, by what power do some of your representatives make people whole? Are your healers also demonic? However, if I overcome the demonic by the Spirit of God, then the Spirit dimension has been demonstrated to you.

"But consider one more question: How can you break into a strong man's house and steal his valuables, except first you conquer the man? When you have conquered him, then you can take what you want from him. Do you now understand the relationship I have with the demonic? Whoever is not cooperating with me in the conquest of the demonic opposes me. Whoever does not work with me toward unity, wholeness, and fulfillment is creating division and destruction. I tell you that persons can have all kinds of failure forgiven, even experiences of making holy things common, but they will not be forgiven for making the Holy Spirit common. For example, if anyone accuses the Representative Man of evil, that can be forgiven. But if anyone continually opposes the Holy Spirit, that opposition cannot be forgiven, in this era or in the one coming.

"Get your life in union with God and let your behavior demonstrate it, or else your life will get completely out of control and your behavior will show it. People's inner lives are recognized by their behavior. So many of you listening to me are self-deluded pretenders. When you are out of union with God, how can you talk about what is good? Don't you realize that the words that come out of your mouth express your innermost being? If your behavior is good, it is because you are drawing out of an inner union with God. If your behavior is destructive, it is likewise because you are acting from a distorted or confused relationship with God. Truly, I tell you that every word you speak is an indicator of your relationship with God, and for this you are accountable. So what you say symbolizes how it is between you and God; your words point either toward wholeness or toward destruction."

SEEK NEW LIFE, NOT MIRACLES

The group of observers from the rule keepers said, "Teacher, show us some miracles." Immediately he reacted, saying, "Only a group of persons who are cut off from their roots and have become fascinated with magic want to see a miracle. There is only one miracle that you will see, and it is the one that Jonah, the spokesperson of old, symbolizes. As this ancient spokesperson spent three days and nights in a big fish, so the Representative Man will spend three days and three nights in the earth's belly. The citizens of that ancient city of Nineveh will reproach you on the day of reckoning, because they changed their attitudes and lifestyle under the teaching of Jonah. And a more significant person than Jonah has spoken to you. Also the pagan queen who came out of the South to visit Solomon will accuse you on that day of reckoning. She came a long way to hear Solomon's wisdom, yet I say to you a person greater than Solomon has spoken wisdom to you.

"When a negative, unproductive way of life has been repressed, that old pattern is not abolished nor destroyed but hangs around looking for a way to return and take over your life. One day that pattern, which has such great strength, says, 'I will return to that person where I lived for so long and see if he or she has replaced me with another way of life.' If a new style has not replaced the old, unproductive one, a strange thing will happen. That old pattern will return with seven times the power it previously had and will be more destructive than it was originally. The final condition of that person is far worse than the former. And that's how it will be with a whole generation of persons who do not find their center in God."

MATTHEW 12:22–45

DAY 25

JESUS DESCRIBES THE SPIRIT DIMENSION

He told them another story: "The Spirit dimension is like a farmer who planted good seed in his field. While that farmer slept, an enemy of his went through his field sowing weeds among the good seed and then went on his way. When the good seed first sprouted and came up, the wheat it produced didn't look any different from the weeds. Later on, however, the weeds became apparent. So one day, the farmhands said to their employer, 'Didn't you sow good seed in the fields? Where did these weeds come from?' The farmer answered, 'An enemy of mine has done this.' The farmhands said, 'Do you want us to pull up the weeds?' 'No,' said the farmer, 'while you are pulling up the weeds, you may also pull up the wheat, and I would lose the whole crop. Let the weeds and the wheat grow together until harvesttime. When we are harvesting, I will instruct you reapers to gather the weeds, bale them, and burn them up, but store the wheat in the barn.'"

He spoke still another story to them: "The Spirit dimension is like a small package of yeast with which a woman mixed three cups of flour, and it yeasted all the flour."

That day, Jesus told all these stories to the crowd, and he didn't say anything to them that was not in story form. Again, this mode of speaking had been forecast by one of God's servants long ago, who said, "I will speak to you in stories; I will articulate mysteries that have been hidden from the creation of the world."

When he finished speaking, Jesus dismissed the crowd and walked back over to his house. On the way, his understudies said, "Will you explain to us the story about the weeds in the field?" Jesus responded, "The one who planted the good seed is the Representative Man. The field is the world, and the good seeds are the persons already born into the Spirit dimension, but weeds are those persons who have chosen another source for their lives. The enemy that directs them is the Adversary. The harvest points to the climax of history, and those who do the gathering and separating are God's workers. As those weeds are baled and burned in the fire, that's how it will be at the climax of history. The Representative Man will commission his followers to separate out those persons who have not been open to the Spirit dimension and have thus blocked its expansion. And the pain felt by those who are separated will be like burning in a fire, and there will be much sorrow. After that, those who have a right relationship with God will glow in the presence of their Father like the radiance of the sun. If you have ears, then listen to what I am saying.

"The Spirit dimension can also be compared to a trunk of gold buried in a field. If a person should inadvertently discover that trunk, he or she would cover it up and eagerly sell everything to buy the field in which the treasure is hidden.

"The Spirit dimension is also like a jeweler seeking precious stones. When he finds one jewel that is worth an enormous sum of money, he will liquidate all his other holdings to purchase it. Also, the Spirit dimension can be compared to a large net that is dropped into a lake and gathers fish of all kinds. When that net is full, the fishers draw it to shore and sit down, separating the fish that are worth keeping from those that are not. A similar separation will take place at the climax of history, when God's messengers will separate the true participants in the Spirit dimension from the pretenders. And the sense of loss that those pretenders experience will be unbearable."

Jesus then questioned his understudies: "Do you understand what I am talking about?" They all nodded. "Yes, yes, we do." Then he said to them, "Every person who understands the principles of the Spirit dimension is like a home owner who has both precious antiques and modern furnishings—she or he can always display something new."

MATTHEW 13:24–30, 33–52

"Spend your energy looking not for food which is temporal but rather for the food that lasts for ever and ever. I am speaking of the food that the Representative Man can give you, because God the Father has authorized him to do just that." Thinking of the healings they had observed and the huge crowd, they asked Jesus, "How can we do these mighty works of God that you are doing?" Jesus stated simply, "The work of God is for you to trust the one whom God has sent into the world." They asked him, "What proof do you offer us that we can trust you? What works do you do? We recall how our ancestors ate food in the desert. It's written in our records, 'Moses gave them bread from heaven to eat.'"

Jesus said to them, "I tell you the truth, it is not Moses who gave you the bread from heaven but it is my Father who gives you the true bread from heaven. For the food God offers is the person who has come from God and offers life to the whole world."

The crowd demanded, "Well, sir, give us this food. In fact, keep on giving it to us." Then Jesus said plainly, "I am the food that gives life. The person who enters into a relationship with me will never hunger, and the person who trusts in me will never be thirsty. Truly, all of you have seen me, but not all of you trust me. Some will trust me, and those whom the Father turns toward me I will never reject. I came out of the immediate presence of God to do what God purposes and not to initiate a purpose of my own. And it is the Father's purpose that I forfeit not one person or thing given to me, so that all will be fulfilled on the day of ultimate fulfillment. I say to you clearly, the one who commissioned me wills authentic life age after age for those who trust in me, and I will fulfill them completely on the day of the ultimate fulfillment."

At that, the crowd began whispering and complaining because he said, "I am the food that has come from the presence of God." They reacted, "Isn't this Jesus, Joseph's son? Don't we know his mother and father? How can he claim to have come from the presence of God?" Sensing what was going on, Jesus said, "Stop whispering and complaining to each other. None will enter into a relationship with me unless my Father draws them into it. I will fulfill them on the day of the ultimate fulfillment. God's spokespersons said, 'Everyone will be instructed by God.' Every person then who hears, who is instructed by my Father, will become aware of this relationship with me. Now, no human being has ever envisioned the Father except the one who has come from the immediate presence of God; he has seen the Father. Again, I tell you truthfully, the person who trusts me experiences authentic life age after age. I myself am the food of life.

Your ancestors ate food in the desert. They are now dead. I am talking to you about the food that comes from the presence of God. A person can eat it and never die. I am the living food which came from the presence of God. If people eat this food, they will participate in life forever. Now, the food I am offering is my flesh, my very life, and I will give my life for the life of the world."

This saying completely perplexed the Jews. They struggled with each other again, asking, "How can a human being like this man give us his flesh to eat?" With no explanation, Jesus continued, "I am telling you the truth—unless you eat the flesh of the Representative Man and drink his blood, you have no life in you. Whoever partakes of my flesh and drinks my blood has authentic life age after age and will be fulfilled on the day of ultimate fulfillment. My flesh is truly food, and my blood is truly drink. The person who eats my flesh and drinks my blood has the most intimate relationship with me imaginable. I am in that person and that person is in me. Just as I have come from the presence of the living God and experience life from my Father, so the person who eats me will experience life through me. You see, I am describing the food that comes from the presence of God, a food unlike that eaten by your fathers, who died. The person who eats this food will live forever." This is what he taught in the Jewish house of worship in Capernaum, where he had made his headquarters.

When many of his understudies heard this discourse, they talked among themselves, saying, "This is a difficult teaching. Who can understand it?" When Jesus recognized that his followers were struggling with his teaching, he said to them, "Is this difficult for you to accept? What will you do when you witness the Representative Man going back into the immediate presence of God? Remember that the Spirit gives life. Human striving cannot achieve it. The symbols I use to describe reality participate in the Spirit of God and release life within you. But even among you there are some who do not trust me." Jesus had known all along who did not trust him, and he even knew who would betray him. "That's why I have said to you," he continued, "that no person can enter into a relationship with me unless it is given that person by my Father."

After that, a number of those who had associated with him withdrew from their relationship with him. As they were leaving, Jesus turned to the twelve he had chosen, asking, "Will you also withdraw from your relationship with me?" Immediately, Simon Peter answered, "Sir, where would we go? You alone have described to us the authentic life, which lasts forever. We trust you. We are certain that you are the Messiah, the Son of the living God." But Jesus responded, "I have chosen you twelve to be in an intimate fellowship with me, and one of you is my adversary." Jesus was describing Judas Iscariot, the son of Simon, because he was the member of the inner circle who would hand him over to his enemies.

JOHN 6:27–71

DAY 26

EMPTY RITUALS

Then several pious rule keepers and interpreters came from Jerusalem to interview Jesus. They observed with a critical spirit that Jesus' understudies did not practice the customary ritual of hand washing before eating. These pious rule keepers and interpreters do not put food into their mouths unless they go through this hand-washing ritual; neither do Jews of any sect, for that matter, because they have a special loyalty to "the way we have always done it." For example, if one of them has been to the market, he will not eat unless he first goes through the washing ritual. In addition to the hand-washing ceremony, they have a variety of washings they practice: washing pots and pans and tables and so on.

These pious men quizzed Jesus: "Why do your understudies disregard the traditions our fathers passed on to us? Why don't they observe the hand-washing ritual before they eat?" Jesus responded, "Isaiah perfectly described you pretenders when he said, 'This group affirms me verbally, but their words are cut off from their feelings and actions. Empty is this group's attempt at communion with me, because their faith is nothing more than human fabrication.' You have disregarded the clear directives of God in favor of these traditional ways of living—like washing hands and pots and pans." Jesus spoke explicitly: "Very clearly you are rejecting God's rule in order to keep doing what you have always done, in the way you have always done it. Let me point to one of your practices to illustrate what I mean. Moses, as God's spokesperson, said, 'Respect and care for your father and mother, because whoever dishonors his parents will suffer the consequences.' You nullify God's directive by your humanly created ritual. For example, if your parents have needs, you make a pronouncement over your resources—'This is dedicated to God'—and by your ritual deny your parents what they need. With this ritual, you free yourself from responsibility for your parents. With your homemade excuse, you nullify God's rule. This is but one example of the numerous ways you set aside God's directives to preserve your cultural practices."

At this point in the discussion, Jesus invited the crowd to come in closer. "Listen to me, every one of you, listen, understand what I have to say! Nothing outside people that enters into their awareness or experience can cause distortion or contamination. But what originates in the inner being of persons and comes out through their actions—this contaminates. If you grasp what I am saying, appropriate this truth for your life."

When Jesus entered the house to relax a bit, his understudies asked him to explain his statement. "Do you not grasp the significance of these ideas?" he asked. "Don't you see that what enters into a person cannot contaminate because it is neither good nor bad in itself? Things on the outside do not enter the feelings and motivations but rather go into the stomach and pass into the intestines and out as waste." (This statement indicates that food and drink have no moral significance, so what persons eat or drink does not define who they are.) Jesus continued, "The behavior that originates in a person's inner being can contaminate him or her. From the inside, out of the depths of a person, comes destructive behavior: negative thinking, sex of any kind without commitment, destruction of the lives of others, taking or coveting another's goods, blindness to others' needs, game playing, undisciplined expression of every desire, paranoid behavior, irreverence toward holy things, arrogance and pride, thoughtless or meaningless action—all these destructive actions come from the depths of a person and are motivated from the inner being. Functioning in these ways contaminates and destroys a person."

MARK 7:1–23

JESUS CAUSES CONTROVERSY

Jesus traveled around in his home district of Galilee; because certain Jews were seeking to kill him, he could not stay in Jerusalem or the surrounding area. About this time, the Jews were preparing to celebrate the time when their ancestors lived in tents during the desert wanderings. Realizing that the festival was about to take place, Jesus' brothers ironically suggested, "Why don't you go up to Judea, so that your followers there may see the spectacular works you do? The person seeking recognition and acclaim doesn't perform spectacular works in secret but rather shows himself to everyone. If you are doing such phenomenal acts, then let everyone see them." (Remember, his brothers did not believe he was God's special representative.) But Jesus responded, "It is not the appropriate time for me to show myself to the crowd, but any time is all right for you to go to the festival. Those persons separated from God's purpose are not hostile to you, but they are to me. And they're reacting to me because I am pointing out the motives that underlie their behavior. So why don't you go on up to the festival? I am not planning to go at this time, because it is not the proper moment." After this conversation with his brothers, he remained in Galilee.

After his brothers departed for the festival, however, Jesus also set out on the journey. He did not publicize his trip but traveled incognito. During the festival, a number of leading Jews asked, "Where is he?" There was also a volatile debate between opposing segments in the crowd. Some said, "He is a sincere, honest person." Others said, "No, he is manipulative and deceptive." Yet with all the talk, not a single person claimed faith in Jesus, because all feared the consequences.

DAY 27

JESUS' AUTHORITY IS FROM GOD

When the festival was about half over, Jesus went into God's house and began teaching. The Jews in authority were shocked. They said, "How does this man know what he is talking about? He has never attended the school of the rabbis." Jesus explained, "The teaching I offer does not originate in me. Rather, I am expressing the mind of the one who sent me. If any person acts in accordance with God's will, the source of my teaching will become clear—that is, whether it originates in God or in me. If what I'm saying originates in me, then I am seeking recognition and acclaim for myself. But if I am looking for the recognition and acclaim of God, who commissioned me, then I am authentic, and there is no contradiction. You

---

Jesus the Son of God

In the life of Jesus, several occurrences give us the impression that we are dealing with someone who is a different kind of human being. We never get the impression that he was a spirit from heaven who did not possess a human body like ours, but there are hints that he is more than an "ordinary" man. For example, consider the narrative of his birth.

A heavenly messenger startled his mother, Mary, with the news that the Spirit of God would act on her body and she would conceive a child.

(continued)

all claim allegiance to Moses. He gave you the rules, but none of you keeps them. If you are keeping them, why are you trying to kill me?"

The crowd shouted, "You're crazy! Who's trying to kill you?" Then Jesus said, "I have made someone well on your sacred day, and all of you are shocked. Let me point out your contradiction. Moses commended to you the right of circumcision. (Actually, it did not originate with Moses but with our common ancestors.) If the day for a boy's circumcision falls on the sacred day, you will perform that ritual. If you're willing to circumcise a male child on the sacred day to keep the rule that Moses laid down, why are you so hostile to me because I made a person whole on the sacred day? I wish you would evaluate me according to my motives and not according to your tradition and culture."

Some from Jerusalem began to whisper, "Isn't this the man they're trying to kill? Look how he presents himself openly. None of the rulers are saying anything to him. Do they really think this is the Christ? Why, we know this man! We know where he came from and all about him, but when the Christ appears, no one will know all about him."

DIVIDED OPINIONS ABOUT JESUS

As Jesus was teaching in God's house, his voice grew stronger as he declared, "You do know my name. You even know where I was born and where I live. Yet I have not appeared of my own choice and will; I have been sent by one who is genuine and real. You don't know him, but I do. I originated in him, and I have been appointed and commissioned by him."

With that statement, the leaders tried to take Jesus captive. But mysteriously, they could not capture him, because the appropriate time had not come. While some were seeking to kill him, others trusted him. They said,

---

Mary, a virgin, was engaged to Joseph, a descendant of King David of Israel. God's special messenger came to Mary saying, "Greetings! You have been especially chosen. The Lord is with you in a special way." The greeting baffled her and filled her with anxiety, and she wondered what it meant.

Then the messenger said, "Don't be anxious, Mary, for you have found a special place with God. I have come to tell you that you will conceive a son and give birth to Jesus, who will be recognized as the Son of God."

We do not know how all this happened, but we do know that Mary

(continued)

"When Christ appears, will he do anything more phenomenal than we have already seen this man do?" When the pious rule keepers realized that some of the people were beginning to have confidence in Jesus, they joined forces with the religious authorities to arrest him.

Jesus continued his teaching: "I am going to be in your midst a little while longer, and then I will return to the one who appointed and commissioned me. You will look for me, and you will not find me. Where I go, you cannot accompany me." Because this statement was puzzling to the Jews, they began asking themselves, "Where will he go so that we can't find him? Does this mean he will go to the non-Jews and teach them? What does this strange saying mean, 'You will look for me and you will not find me,' and also 'Where I'm going, you cannot come'?"

On the very last day of the festival, when the crowd was the largest and the celebration was at its peak, in full view of all, Jesus said, "If your life is arid and meaningless, and you thirst for real being, I invite you to enter into a relationship with me that will be like a drink of life. Those who enter into a trust relationship with me will experience real life flowing out of their inner being, just as our records have predicted." In this statement, Jesus was alluding to the Spirit that would be poured into the lives of all who entered into a trust relationship with him. However, at this time the Holy Spirit was not fully active, because Jesus had not returned into the immediate presence of God.

When the crowd heard his declaration, many responded, "Certainly, this is a spokesperson for God." Others even said, "This is the Messiah." Still others questioned, "Will the Messiah come from Galilee? Don't our records state that the Messiah is a descendant of David? And doesn't this mean that he must come from Bethlehem, David's home?" So, because of

---

believed she had been encountered by the other dimension, by God's messenger. She held these memories until years later, when she would tell them to her son and to his followers. From the beginning, Jesus was understood to be the Son of God conceived in Mary's womb.

This special relation Jesus had with God was first manifest at his baptism. At his baptism, an amazing thing happened. When Jesus came up out of the river, the sky opened up and something descended like a dove on to Jesus, and he heard a voice saying, "You are my much loved Son; I am very pleased with you."

(continued)

his statements, there was a division in the crowd's reaction. Skeptics in the crowd were ready to arrest him, but actually, not a person laid a hand on him.

About this time, the religious officials and the rule keepers asked the soldiers, "Why haven't you arrested him?" Defensively, the soldiers explained, "We have never heard a person speak like this before." The pious rule keepers accosted them, saying, "Have you been deluded also? You don't see any of your leaders or any of us keepers of the rules placing confidence in him, do you? These people who don't know our rules and are not versed in our ways are being deceived and led astray."

But Nicodemus, the man who one night had a private interview with Jesus, said, "Do our rules permit us to condemn a person before we hear him and know what he has done?" The leaders answered, "Are you defending him because you are from Galilee? Search our records thoroughly; not a single spokesman of God has come from Galilee." Then the festival was over, and everyone went home.

DAY 28

JESUS PUTS COMPASSION ABOVE LEGALISM

Afterward, Jesus went out to the Mount of Olives to find solitude. The next morning he returned to God's house, and so did the people to whom he had preached. While he was continuing his teaching, the interpreters of the rules and the rule keepers interrupted him. They dragged in a woman who had been caught in the act of adultery, and they seated her before him. With sarcasm in their voices, they said, "Teacher, we caught this woman committing adultery. Moses ruled that we should stone her. What do you

---

As we have seen, this first budding awareness of Jesus' identity as the Son of God met with a severe test. The focus of the testing in the desert to which we have alluded was on his identity as Son of God. Each of the temptations began with "If you are the Son of God . . ." So the struggle in the desert dealt not only with pride, greed, and unbridled passion but with his sense of identity, his confidence about being the Son of God.

This aspect of Jesus' person received further confirmation on the mountaintop, in the experience he had with three of his followers (see

(continued)

say?" Actually, they were forcing this encounter so that they could drum up a charge against Jesus. Apparently paying no attention to them, Jesus leaned over and with his finger began writing in the sand. They persisted in their questioning and demanded that he answer them. Finally, he looked up and said, "Will the perfect one among you throw the first stone, please?"

As Jesus continued writing in the sand, these manipulators felt immense guilt, and they began leaving. The oldest left first, followed by the others. Finally, there remained only Jesus and the woman standing before him. At last, Jesus looked up at her. Compassionately he asked, "My dear, what happened to those who were making a case against you? Is no one left to point an accusing finger at you?" "No," she replied. "Then," said Jesus, "I don't accuse or condemn you either. Go now and live like a true child of God."

JESUS ESTABLISHES HIS PURPOSE

After this episode, Jesus continued his teaching: "I illuminate the meaning of life. The person who enters into a relationship with me will no longer live in meaninglessness but will have the clue to the meaning of life." To this clear statement about his identity the rule keepers reacted, "You yourself are telling us who you are, but it is improper for a person to affirm himself. Others must affirm you." Jesus asserted, "Yes, I am telling you who I am, and what I say is accurate. I know where I have come from, what I am doing here, and where I am going. And you don't know where I have come from or where I am going. You are judging me according to human standards and by human wisdom. I do not make judgments. But if I should judge another, my judgment would be accurate, because I would not make it in and of myself but rather out of my union with the Father, who has chosen and commissioned me.

---

page 94) as a voice spoke to them from the cloud: "This is my son; listen to him."

In addition to these occurrences, statements that Jesus made that arose in own consciousness point to his relationship with God. Jesus claimed to be one with God: "The Father and I are one" (John 10:30). To be one with God means to be unified, one in spirit, aim, and being. In conversation with one of his followers, Jesus said, "If you know me, you will know my Father also" (John 14:7). This was—and is—an astounding statement.

(continued)

"Incidentally, you should recall that in your rules truth is established by the agreement of two witnesses. I have told you very clearly who I am, and the Father who has commissioned me tells you who I am. That makes two." Still resisting, they asked, "Where is your Father?" Jesus answered, "There is no way I can describe the Father to you since you don't recognize me or him. If you had recognized me, you would have immediately known who my Father is." Jesus taught all these things in the treasury room of God's house. And no one arrested him, because his time had not yet been fulfilled. "I will fulfill the purpose for which I came into the world," Jesus told them. "Though you will look for me, you will eventually die in your estrangement from God. Where I am going, you cannot follow me." This statement really puzzled the Jews, and they began asking among themselves, "Will he commit suicide?" They raised this question because he said, "Where I am going, you cannot follow me." Jesus said, "You were born naturally, but my origin is with God. You belong to the natural process of things and experience life as an end in itself, but I live for the final purpose and ultimate goal of creation. And I said that you would die in your isolation from God because you do not trust that I am the Messiah; therefore, you will continue in your present condition of alienation." Then they asked him, "Just who are you?" Jesus said, "My answer is the same that I have given you time and again from the beginning of my ministry. There are so many things I wish to clarify for you. But out of faithfulness to the one who commissioned me, I reveal only what I have been told." They didn't understand that he was referring to God.

Still reasoning with them, Jesus said, "When you have lifted up God's Representative Man, as Moses lifted up the snake, at that time you will recognize that I am the one you have been looking for. Then you will become

In this person who was a teacher and miracle worker in a small country of the Middle East, the divine mystery, God, personified and particularized himself. This suggests that if we want to know what God is like, what God wills, and the manner of knowing God, we must look at Jesus Christ.

Jesus said, "I am the way, and the truth, and the life. No one comes to the Father except through me" (John 14:6). This radical statement that Jesus Christ provides the way to God and that apart from him persons cannot come to God indicates the uniqueness of Jesus.

(continued)

aware that I am not initiating a private movement of my own, but as my Father has taught me, I am teaching you. I am confident that the one who selected me and commissioned me is with me. My Father has not forsaken me, and I always do what pleases him." As he was saying these things, many persons trusted him.

DAY 29

HERITAGE IS NOT ENOUGH

Then Jesus addressed the Jews who had trusted him: "If you appropriate my teaching, you will demonstrate that you are truly my understudies. Furthermore, as you express my teaching in your lives, you will discover the truth, and the truth will liberate you to be the persons God destined you to be." The Jews argued, "We are the offspring of Abraham. We have never been enslaved to anyone. What do you mean, 'We will be free to be the persons God destined us to be'?" Making it clear that he was not referring to physical slavery, Jesus said, "I tell you the truth, whoever sins is a slave to sin. And you know from experience that the slave does not always have free access to his owner's house, but the son of the slave owner does. I'm saying that if the Son liberates you, you will be truly liberated. I am aware that you are Abraham's offspring, and you are trying to kill me because what I'm teaching does not stick to you. It seems very simple: I am speaking what I have learned from observing my Father, and you are doing what you have observed from your father."

Hostile and defensive, they argued, "Abraham is our father." Jesus responded, "If you were truly Abraham's offspring, you would live the kind of life Abraham did. But instead, you are trying to kill me, trying to kill a

---

In our efforts to be faithful followers of Christ, some of us, in the years since his life and work on earth, may have been too eager to restrict his activity to our limited understanding. Being the way, the truth, and the life may mean that, in ways we have never imagined, Jesus works in history, culture, and other religions to bring persons into a relationship with God.

We do not claim that Jesus has been captured by the Christian community and confined in its dogma and liturgy. We believe that he is indeed in the midst of the community called church but that he is also

(continued)

person who has told you the truth, which I have heard from Abraham's God. Abraham didn't function like that. You are doing what your father inspires." They persisted, "We are not illegitimate children. We have one Father, God." Jesus continued the debate: "If God were your Father, you would relate to me in love, because I have come from God. I didn't choose to come. I was sent. Why can't you understand what I am saying? I suppose it's because you can't grasp my analogies. Let me try again. You are under the control of your father, the Adversary. You are doing the desires of your father, who has always been a murderer. He has never participated in the truth because no truth is in him. Besides, he is deceitful, and when he lies, he is expressing his true nature. He has always lied and is the source of lies. In contrast, I speak the truth to you and you won't believe it. Can any of you prove that I am estranged from God? If I am in union with God and speak accurately about God, why don't you believe me? Persons united to God recognize God's words; you don't recognize them because you are not in a positive relationship with God."

The Jews then asked, "Don't you realize you are an outcast and crazy?" Jesus responded, "I am not crazy, nor am I an outcast. Rather, I respect my Father and you disrespect me. I am not searching for power and recognition, but my Father gives it to me anyway. Again, let me say the truth to you: if a person embraces what I am saying and expresses it in his life, he will not die." To that, the Jews said, "We are now positive that you are crazy. Abraham is dead. God's spokespersons are dead. You say, 'If a man embraces what I am teaching, he will never experience death.' Do you think you are more important than our father Abraham, who is dead? Or God's spokespersons who are dead? Just who do you think you are?" Jesus answered, "If I am generating this esteem out of myself, my esteem

---

in the world seeking to awaken all persons, to open the eyes of all who are blind, to heal all who are sick, and to raise to new awareness and life those who are dead.

We do not exclude his light from other religions. Cannot the way, the truth, and the life be hinted at and suggested in other faiths? Must we believe that only our lamp shines with the light of God? Everything true in other religions reveals Christ; even the thoughts and actions of those who do not even know him in a mysterious way embody him. But we

(continued)

becomes worthless. But it is my Father who esteems me, and you claim that he is your God. Yet you have never really known him. I do know him. If I should say, 'I don't know him,' I'd be a liar just like you; but I do know him, and I live in accordance with his purpose. Even your father Abraham celebrated my birth. He saw it a long time ago and rejoiced over it." Still the Jews argued, "You are not even fifty years old, and you have seen Abraham?" Then Jesus really astounded them by saying, "I tell you the truth, that before Abraham lived, I was living." With that, they grabbed up stones and began pelting Jesus. He hid from them and slipped out of God's house, passing through the crowd to get away.

DAY 30

PHYSICAL AND SPIRITUAL BLINDNESS

On another day in his travels, Jesus met a man who had been born blind. Thinking his blindness was punishment for sin, the understudies asked Jesus, "Teacher, for whose sin is this man being punished? His parents or his own?" "Neither," Jesus observed. "Rather, this progression of creation offers God another opportunity to reveal himself. I must continue to participate in God's creative process while I have the opportunity, because the time is coming when neither I nor anyone else will be able to. While I am present on earth, I reveal the meaning of life." With those words, Jesus made a pack from clay and saliva and put it on the eyes of the blind man. Then he instructed the man, "Go to the pool of Siloam and wash this clay off your eyes." (Jesus sent him to a pool whose name means "sent.") The man went and washed and returned with his eyes open.

The first response to him was from his neighbors and others who had

---

do believe that he is the measuring stick for all truth about God. In short, *God is like Jesus!*

Who is Jesus? We have looked at the announcement of his birth and at the voice that spoke at his baptism and on the mountain, and we have listened to those claims that Jesus made about himself. We conclude this aspect of our inquiry with what one of his followers had to say about him.

On one occasion, Jesus asked his band of followers, "Who do you say that I am?" Without hesitation Simon Peter, the big fisherman who was on the mountain with him when the cloud and voice came, blurted out:

(continued)

seen him begging daily. They inquired, "Isn't this the beggar who used to be blind?" Some said yes, while others said, "He just looks like him." But the man himself stated plainly, "I am he." With that they quizzed him, "How did you receive your sight?" He related his story simply: "A man whom they called Jesus made a mud pack, put it on my eyes, and told me, 'Go wash this off in the pools of Siloam.' And I went and washed it off and my eyes were opened." Probing further, they asked, "Where is this man?" And he answered, "I don't know."

These interrogators took the man who had been blind to the rule keepers. It was on the Jewish sacred day that Jesus made the clay and restored the man's sight. Then they questioned the man, asking, "How did you receive your sight?" He gave them the same answer: "This man put a mud pack on my eyes, and when I washed it off, I could see." The rule keepers reacted angrily, saying, "This man did not come out of the immediate presence of God because he does not honor the sacred day." Again there was division, because some of the crowd said, "This man is not in harmony with God. How can he make a blind man see?" The rule keepers continued to query the man who had been blind: "What do you say about this man who opened your eyes?" Without any hesitation, he declared, "He is from God."

Unwilling to accept the man's statement that he had been born blind, the Jews had his parents brought in. They asked them, "Is this your son, and was he born blind? How is he able to see today?" The man's parents answered discreetly, "We know that this man is our son. He was born blind. How he is able to see today, we don't know. We don't know who opened his eyes. But since he is of legal age, ask him. He can speak for himself." The man's parents spoke cautiously because they feared the Jewish leaders. They were aware these officials had already agreed to exclude from their worship

---

"You are the Messiah, the unique representative of God who is alive and active among us."

Jesus affirmed his answer: "You're experiencing the fulfillment, Simon, son of John; you did not arrive at that answer by logic or reason. Only my Father could have given you that answer."

Months after this confession, Peter stood before the Jewish council explaining a miracle of healing that had occurred on a lame man. Part of his witness to them included these words: "There is no other name given under heaven among humankind whereby we must be saved." At

(continued)

anyone who acknowledged Jesus was the Messiah. That's the reason his parents said, "Since he is of legal age, ask him yourself."

Once again, the leaders called the man who had been blind and instructed him, "Honor God and say this man is a sinner." But he answered, "I don't know whether he is a sinner or not. I just know one thing. I used to be blind, and now I can see." Again they quizzed him, "What exactly did he do? How was he able to make you see?" Again the man answered, "I have already told you how he made me see, and you didn't hear me. Do you want me to tell you again so that you can become his followers?" They recoiled at his retort and exclaimed, "You may be his follower, but we are followers of Moses. We are certain that Moses was a spokesperson of God. We don't have any idea who this man is."

The man answered, "I find your response rather puzzling, because he has done an act of mercy by opening my eyes, which were blind, and you don't know where he is coming from! We have always been taught that God does not hear sinners, but if anyone worships God and does what God wants, God hears that person. Have you ever before heard of someone who was born blind receiving sight? If this man, Jesus, did not originate in God, he could not open the eyes of a person who was born blind." In rage, the leaders attacked him, saying, "You were born in sin, and do you think you can instruct us?" And with that, they threw him out of God's house.

News of this rejection came to Jesus, and when he had found the man he said, "Do you trust the Representative Man?" He answered, "Who is he, sir, that I may trust him?" Then Jesus said to him, "You have already seen him, and right now he is talking with you." And the man said, "Sir, I trust." And he knelt down in reverence.

Reflecting on the response of the blind man and the Jewish leaders, Jesus

this point, Peter seems to be clear that the way to God is through Jesus of Nazareth, whom he called the Christ.

avowed, "I am present on this earth to bring persons to decision. Those who seem to see will not see, and those who are blind will receive sight." A group of the rule keepers overheard him and asked, "Are we blind?" Jesus said, "If you were blind spiritually, you wouldn't be responsible for your action. But you say, 'We see.' So, you are responsible for your sin."

DAY 31

THE TRUSTWORTHY SHEPHERD

"I tell you the truth, if a person does not enter the sheepfold through the door but forces his way in by other means, that person is like a burglar breaking into a house. The shepherd, in contrast, always enters through the door. The keeper of the sheepfold opens the door to him. The sheep recognize the tone of his voice, and he recognizes each sheep, calls each by name, and guides them all. When he puts his sheep out to pasture, he walks in front of them; the sheep follow him, because they know him. The sheep will not follow a stranger but will run away, because they do not recognize the voice of strangers." Jesus told this story with its depth of meaning, but his listeners did not understand it.

Jesus then spoke more clearly. "I tell you the truth—I am the door through which the sheep enter. All of those who came before me were burglars, but the sheep did not follow them. I myself am the door. Persons who enter life through me will be safe; I will nurture them and give them freedom. Burglars are dishonest, murderous, and destructive. But I am here to offer life, even life beyond what you have ever known. I am the trustworthy shepherd. A trustworthy shepherd will die for his sheep. But if a person is just hired for the job and is not really committed to the sheep, when a wolf attacks, that person will run away and leave the sheep. The wolf will catch some and frighten others. You see, the hired help runs away because that person is a deceiver and is not genuinely concerned about the sheep. I am a trustworthy shepherd. I recognize all my sheep, and my sheep recognize me. My relation to the sheep is like my relation with the Father. He knows me and I know him, and I will die for my sheep. Incidentally, I have another breed of sheep that don't belong to this fold. I must also round them up, for they will respond to me. Eventually there will be only one flock and one shepherd. I am confident of my

Suggestion #9

You have read the stories of Jesus' birth, healing, and teaching. Consider his question to you: "Now, who do you say that I am?"

Father's love. And because of that, I will offer my life, but it will be given back to me. Many are trying to kill me, yet no one can take my life away from me. However, I offer it freely because I have the authority both to offer my life and then to receive it back again. This is the promise my Father has given me."

JESUS CLAIMS ONENESS WITH THE FATHER

When Jesus finished the story, there was a split among the Jews concerning him. One group said, "This man's the devil. Poor fellow, he's crazy. Why should we be paying any attention to him?" Another group countered, "A man who's crazy doesn't talk or act like this. Can a devil open blind eyes?"

Later on, during the winter, Jesus was in Jerusalem at another celebration of the Jews. While he was there, he walked through God's house, through the part that is called Solomon's porch. Again, a crowd of Jews gathered around him and asked, "How long will you keep us waiting? If you are the Messiah, tell us clearly." Jesus said, "I've already told you, and you didn't believe me. My actions, which are inspired by my Father, tell you who I am. You did not believe my words or my deeds because you don't belong to me. You are not my sheep. The sheep that belong to me recognize my voice, and I recognize them and they follow me. I give my followers life forever, so that they will never die; no one will be able to destroy their relationship with me. My Father, who gave me a relationship with them, is greater than everyone and everything, and no one will be able to destroy their relationship with him. I am in perfect and complete union with my Father."

With that, the Jews grabbed up stones to kill him. Jesus answered, "I have done a number of good deeds that reveal my Father. Now, for which of these are you trying to kill me?" The Jews answered quickly, "It's not for the good things you have done that we are trying to kill you but because you are blasphemous. You are just a man, and you are claiming to be God." "Haven't you read what is written in your own records, 'I have said you are gods'?" Jesus queried. Indeed, Jesus did call those "gods" who received God's word. "And you trust the scripture, don't you?" he continued. "My Father has set me apart and commissioned me to come to you, and you accuse me of irreverent speech because I said, 'I am God's Son.' If I don't behave as my Father would, don't trust me. But if I do, even if you don't trust what I say, trust what I do. I want you to trust me, so that you may be confident that the Father lives in me and I live in him." Once again, they tried to arrest him, but he escaped.

This time, Jesus went across the Jordan River, where John had baptized, and stayed there. While he was there, many persons came to him. In their conversations they defended Jesus, saying, "Even though John did not perform any miraculous feats, everything he said about this man has proved true." In this out-of-the-way place, many persons trusted in him.

DAY 32

JESUS' POWER OVER DEATH

Jesus had a friend whose name was Lazarus, who lived with his sisters, Mary and Martha, in Bethany, a small village near Jerusalem. His sister Mary was the one who had poured the perfume on Jesus and wiped his feet with her hair. Lazarus's two sisters sent a message to Jesus, saying, "Your very good friend is sick." When Jesus received the message, he responded, "The purpose of this illness is not his death, but rather the fulfillment of God, and God's Son will also be fulfilled through the events that follow." Jesus deeply loved Martha, Mary, and Lazarus, but even after he got the message about Lazarus's illness, he stayed two more days where he was teaching.

Then he said to his understudies, "Let's return to Judea." Fearfully, his followers asked, "Teacher, the last time we were there, the Jewish leaders tried to kill you. Are you sure you want to go back?" Jesus replied, "There are about twelve hours of daylight. When persons walk in the daylight, they don't stumble over rocks in their pathway, because they have natural light. However, if a person walks after dark, he stumbles over those same obstacles because he does not generate light in himself."

He went on to tell them, "Our good friend Lazarus is asleep. I am going now to wake him up." But his understudies misunderstood, saying, "Sir, it's OK for him to be asleep. Why would you awaken him?" Jesus was actually describing the death of Lazarus, but his understudies thought he was talking about normal sleep. Realizing this, Jesus said plainly, "Lazarus is dead. Because of my relationship to you, I am really glad I was not there, since from this you may trust more deeply. Now, let's get going." Then Thomas, who was one of the twins, beckoned the others, saying, "Let's go up with him and die like Lazarus."

By the time Jesus arrived, Lazarus had already been buried in a cave four days. Bethany was just a few miles from Jerusalem. A large number of Jews had already come out to grieve with Martha and Mary. The moment Martha got word that Jesus was on his way, she ran to meet him. Mary remained in the house. "Sir, if you had come when I sent the message, my brother would still be alive," Martha said to Jesus. "But even now, I'm confident that whatever you request of God will be given to you." Jesus promised, "Your brother will experience resurrection and live again." Immediately Martha replied, "I'm aware that he will experience resurrection on the day of the fulfillment of all things." Then Jesus affirmed to her, "I myself am the resurrection and life. The person who trusts me, even though he experiences death, will live. And the person who lives with confidence and trust in me will never experience death. Do you believe this?" "Yes," she answered confidently. "Lord, I believe that you are the Messiah, God's own Son, whom we have been expecting."

With that, she returned to the house and made her way through the mourners to her sister Mary. Martha whispered in her ear, "The teacher has arrived and wants to see you." Immediately, Mary got to her feet and went to Jesus. Jesus had not yet reached the town of Bethany but was waiting outside, where he had conversed with Martha. When Mary arose and left the house, the Jews who had gathered to grieve with her said, "She is going out to the grave to mourn there." So they followed her. When Mary arrived at the place where Jesus was waiting, she looked deeply into his eyes, then fell at his feet, saying, "Lord, if you had only come when we sent the message, my brother would still be alive." When Jesus realized the depth of Mary's grief and the grief of those who were with her, he felt a similar pain himself. "Where have you buried Lazarus?" he asked. They answered, "Sir, come and we will show you." As he followed them, Jesus began weeping. With that, the Jews murmured to one another, "Look how much he cared for him!" And they began questioning among themselves, "If this man could cause a blind man to see, could he not have kept this man from dying?"

When they got to the grave, Jesus felt deep grief. The grave in which Lazarus was buried was a small cave with a stone sealing the entrance. Jesus instructed some of the bystanders, "Roll the stone away." Martha said, "Sir, he's been dead for four days, and by now the body has begun to smell." "Didn't I tell you that if you would trust me, you would see the fulfillment of God?" Jesus responded. So they rolled away the stone, opening the cave. Jesus looked up into the sky and prayed, "My Father, I'm grateful that you have listened to my prayer in the past. I am confident that you always hear me when I pray. But I am praying aloud so that these people may come to trust my witness that you have sent me into the world." When he had concluded his prayer, he shouted loudly, "Lazarus, come out of that grave." And the dead man walked out, his hands and feet still bandaged and a white cloth covering his face. Jesus said to the men who had removed the stone,

"Take the wrappings off him and free him." Many of those Jews who had come to comfort Mary saw what Jesus did and trusted him. But as usual, some did not, and these went to the pious rule keepers and reported what they had seen Jesus do.

THE PLOTTING AGAINST JESUS CONTINUES

This report provoked another gathering of the top religious officials and the rule keepers, who wondered, "What are we going to do? Obviously, this man is doing many marvelous things." One of them suggested, "If we don't stop it, everyone will believe him. And if this precipitates a revolution, the Romans will destroy God's house and our nation." One of the persons in the crowd was Caiaphas, the chief religious official for the year, who answered them, "Don't you realize our plight? It is better for one person to give his life for the people than for our whole nation to be demolished." These words did not arise from him, yet as a special religious leader, Caiaphas unknowingly forecast Jesus' death for the nation. And his forecast included not only the nation but all of God's people scattered abroad. With that justification, the leaders planned how they might put Jesus to death. After that, Jesus was not available to the Jewish leaders but retreated into the desert. He spent most of his time with his understudies in the city of Ephraim.

JOHN 7:1–11:54

DAY 33

JESUS RESTORES SIGHT

They journeyed to Bethsaida. Several residents brought a blind man to Jesus for healing. Jesus took the blind man by the hand and led him outside the town, where he wiped his saliva on the man's eyes and touched them with his fingers. "Can you see anything?" Jesus asked. Looking up from the ground the man said, "I see people, but they look like trees walking around." Jesus touched his eyes again and asked the man to look up. This time he was made whole and saw everyone clearly. Jesus sent him home with clear instructions: "Don't go back into town, and don't tell anyone what I have done for you."

JESUS REVEALS HIS PURPOSE

Jesus left with his understudies and journeyed into the towns of Caesarea Philippi. As they walked along, he asked his followers, "What are the crowds saying about me? Who do they think I am?" They answered, "John the Baptizer; but others say Elijah or one of the old spokespersons for God." "But who do you think I am?" Jesus asked again. Peter responded, "You are the Messiah." And Jesus instructed them, "Do not tell anyone what you have perceived."

MARK 8:22–29

Jesus affirmed, "You're experiencing the fulfillment, Simon, son of John. You did not arrive at that answer by logic or reason. Only my Father could have given you that answer. You are the Rock—and on the rock of your confession I will build an enduring community. The combined forces of evil will not prevail against this community. I will enable you to understand the principles of the Spirit dimension, so that the decisions you make will have far-reaching consequences, blocking some actions while opening others up. The result of your decisions will echo throughout the Spirit dimension." After that conversation, Jesus carefully instructed his followers not to tell anyone that he was the Messiah.

THE WAY IS NOT EASY

Only after his understudies recognized that he was the Messiah did Jesus tell them what he was facing. He explained how he had to go to Jerusalem and be falsely accused and judged by the rulers, the religious leaders, and the interpreters of the rules. He predicted his death and his resurrection on the third day. When Peter realized what he was saying, he pulled Jesus aside and began shouting at him, "This cannot be! You cannot die now!" Then Jesus turned and addressed Peter sternly, "Get away from me, you devil! Your denials offend me because they show you do not understand God's way. You are responding from a typical human perspective."

MATTHEW 16:13–23

WHAT IT MEANS TO JOURNEY WITH JESUS

Then Jesus instructed them more clearly in what it meant to be his understudy. "If any person will accompany me, he must renounce his pseudo-self and daily take an attitude of renunciation toward what is false and superficial. Everyone who focuses on his own security will never find it but will always be anxious. But whoever forfeits his security for my sake, that person will surely have it. Do you suppose anxious persons are making any headway when they accumulate all the wealth in the world and lose their true selves? If they are ultimately rejected, what have they gained? Also, you should know that anyone who is embarrassed about me and my sayings will be embarrassed when I come in the ultimate fulfillment, manifesting the fulfillment of the Father in the company of his dedicated messengers. Actually, I want you to realize that some of you who are listening to me will not experience death until you witness this Spirit dimension breaking in."

CONFIDENCE FOR THE JOURNEY

About eight days later, Jesus took Peter, James, and John and secluded himself with them on the mountain. While he was praying, his countenance appeared to glow with a white light. The light was so bright that his clothes glistened. While he was glowing, two men talked with him—Moses and Elijah. Their countenances also glistened, just as did his, and they talked with him about his death in Jerusalem. Actually, Peter and the other two had gone to sleep, but in the midst of this conversation they awakened and saw the brilliance of Jesus and the two men who were with him. As the two visitors were leaving, Peter said, "Teacher, we have tasted the ultimate fulfillment here. Let us erect three tents so we can stay here—one for you, one for Moses, one for Elijah." Actually, Peter wasn't aware of what he was saying, because he was so excited about what he had seen.

As Peter was speaking, a cloud covered the mountain, and the three understudies were full of fear as they were engulfed in a cloud. While in the cloud, they heard a voice that said, "This is my Son, my chosen one. Listen to what he is saying." When the voice finished and the cloud departed, Jesus was by himself, and those who had witnessed this wonder clung to it in their memory and didn't tell anyone then what they had seen on the mountain.

LUKE 9:23–36

As they made their way down the mountain, Jesus instructed them, "Do not tell anyone about this experience until I am resurrected." Puzzled, the understudies asked, "Why, then, do the interpreters of the rules say that Elijah must come back first?" Jesus explained, "He must come first to get everything ready. But I tell you truthfully that Elijah has already appeared, yet he was not acknowledged and was even mistreated shamefully. That's the way it will be with me." Then Peter, James, and John understood that Jesus was talking about John the Baptizer.

MATTHEW 17:9–13

DAY 34

JESUS UNITES A DIVIDED PERSON

When they joined the other followers, Jesus saw a huge crowd had gathered around them, and the interpreters of the rules were interrogating them. When the crowd saw Jesus, they were struck with awe and ran over to greet him. "Why are you interrogating my followers?" he demanded of the interpreters. Before they could respond, a man in the crowd furnished the answer. "Sir, I brought to you my son who at times seems to be separated from himself, as well as being mute. He seems to be under the power of a separate personality that splits him in two. That divided part causes him to foam at the mouth, gnash his teeth, bite his tongue, and howl like a wild animal. When I asked your followers to make my son whole, they could not."

Jesus said to them all, "O, you unbelieving people, how long must you observe my actions? How long must I endure your lack of faith? Bring your son to me." And they brought the ill lad to Jesus. No sooner was the boy in his presence than he suffered an attack. That other self split off, and the boy fell down on the ground kicking, choking, and screaming. Saliva began running from his mouth. Jesus asked his father, "How long has your son had these seizures?" "Since he was a child," the father responded. "Sometimes this other self tries to destroy him, causing him to fall into the fire or into the water. So if there is anything you can do, please do it, because we desperately need your help." Jesus said, "It is not a question of whether or not I can do anything. Rather, it is a question of whether or not you can believe. Anything can happen if you can believe." Without a thought the father cried out, "I do believe with part of me—help me believe with the other part."

When Jesus realized the crowd was closing in, he said to the child's separated part, "You alienated and destructive part of this boy, I command you to depart and don't trouble him anymore." At those words the boy was thrown into an intense struggle for a few minutes; then the struggle subsided, and the boy relaxed as if he had died. In fact, several in the crowd said, "He is dead." But Jesus took the boy's hand and helped him to his feet. He stood for a moment looking first at Jesus, then at the crowd. Jesus and his understudies left, and when they got inside their home, the understudies asked Jesus, "Why couldn't we make the lad whole?" He answered, "Because this situation requires intense prayer. Nothing else can affect it."

THE TEACHING JOURNEY CONTINUES

Jesus and his understudies continued their journeys, passing through Galilee. Jesus still sought to keep his exact whereabouts a secret. Being aware of the threat against his life, he kept saying to his understudies, "The Representative Man will be handed over to his enemies and finally executed by them. After his execution he will rise from death on the third day." His understudies did not grasp the meaning of "execution" and "rising from death" but were afraid to ask him.

Then John, one of the understudies, said, "Teacher, we observed a man who is not one of us making persons whole in your name. Because he is not an understudy and consequently unqualified, we told him to stop." "Don't stop him," Jesus said. "A person cannot heal in my name and later discount me. If a person does not declare himself against us, he is with us. Anyone who shares with you the least of gifts, such as a cup of water, because you are Christ persons, I tell you the truth—that person will not lose his or her investment."

MARK 9:38–41

When they got back to Capernaum, the tax collectors asked Peter, "Does your teacher pay taxes?" Peter responded, "Of course." When he went into their house, Jesus stopped him and asked, "What do you think, Simon? From whom do governments get their taxes? From their own citizens, or from foreigners?" Peter answered, "They get it from aliens." "Then," said Jesus, "citizens under their government are free of taxation, aren't they? Although we're free, there's no need to create a scene. Go over to the lake and cast a line into the water. Take up the first fish you catch, open his mouth, and in it you will find a piece of money. Take the money to those who collect taxes, and give it to them for me and for you."

A NEW ROUTE TO
RECOGNITION AND FULFILLMENT

About this time, Jesus' understudies came to him, asking, "Who will receive the greatest recognition and power in this new expression of the Spirit dimension?" With that, Jesus looked around in the crowd and found a small child. He beckoned the child and put him down in the midst of them. "I am giving you a clear communication—unless you change your attitude and actions and become like little children, you will not participate in the Spirit dimension. The person who learns to function with the simplicity of a child will receive the greatest recognition and power in the Spirit dimension. And whoever gives unconditional acceptance to the person who lives this way will be giving unconditional acceptance to me. Whoever creates obstacles for a person taking his or her first steps in the Spirit dimension would actually be better off if he had a huge rock tied around his neck and were thrown into the sea. As long as you live in this world, you will face hardship and pain. Those who create these hardships will suffer the consequences of their destructive behavior. Don't create hardship or pain for yourself. If your hand or foot blocks you, get rid of it. It is better to enter life deformed than to be normal and wind up in meaninglessness and despair. And if your eye, for example, blocks your growth, it is better to live with only one eye in this life than to go with two eyes into darkness and everlasting despair.

MATTHEW 17:24–18:9

"Let me talk with you about opening up blocked relationships. Suppose a brother of yours functions in a manner that creates negative feelings in you. Go to your brother and tell him how you feel. If he hears you and cares about your pain, you have deepened your relationship with your brother. If he does not respond to your pain, invite a friend or two to mediate the relationship. Both of you will get a clearer picture when there are other viewpoints. If, under these circumstances, he does not respond, then share your concern with those in your fellowship of faith. If he will not respond to the community of faith, then leave him alone.

"I remind you again that your decisions have far-reaching consequences, whether you are blocking relationships or whether you are opening them up. The result of your efforts reverberates throughout the Spirit dimension. I have told you this before: if two of you can be in harmony concerning something that you really want, ask my Father, the source of all things, and it will happen. And remember, where just two or three of you assemble in my Spirit, I am personally present with you."

DAY 35

JESUS EXPLAINS FORGIVENESS

After that Peter asked Jesus, "How many times am I to forgive my brother when he offends me? Seven?" Jesus responded, "Yes, forgive him seven times, then seventy times seven, or until you lose count.

"Relationships in the Spirit dimension may be compared to a certain banker who was reviewing his debtors. While reviewing their accounts, he found a man who owed him millions of dollars. Because the man did not have any money to pay the note, the banker ordered the court to lock him

-97-

up, along with his wife and children, and to take everything he had. When the debtor realized what was happening, he was shaken to the core of his being and pleaded with the banker, 'Sir, if you will give me time, I promise to pay everything I owe you.' The banker was so moved by the debtor's plea that he told the officer to release him, and he canceled the debt.

"On leaving the bank, that very debtor walked out and found a fellow who owed him a few dollars. He grabbed him, shook him, and began choking him, saying, 'Pay me what you owe me.' And this fellow got down on his knees and begged him, saying, 'If you will just give me a little time, I will repay you every cent I owe you.' His pleas were to no avail, and his fellow had him jailed until he could repay the loan. When some of his neighbors saw what he was doing, they told the banker about it. Then the banker called his debtor again and said, 'You ungrateful and insensitive man! I wiped out the huge loan you owed me because you asked me to. Don't you think that you should have shown tenderness and compassion for your fellow human being, just as I showed compassion to you?' The banker was extremely angry and had the man put into solitary confinement until he paid everything he owed. This story depicts how your heavenly Father will deal with you when you do not forgive your friends and associates."

MATTHEW 18:15–35

THE JOURNEY TO JERUSALEM BEGINS

Later on in his ministry, when it was about time for Jesus to experience his return to heaven, he resolutely determined to go to Jerusalem. To prepare his way, he sent a couple of understudies ahead. They went into a Samaritan village to prepare his reception. When he got to the city, however, they didn't welcome him because he appeared determined to go to Jerusalem. James and John reacted to their rejection with anger. "Lord," they asked "do you want us to make fire rain from the sky and burn them up?" But Jesus rebuked them, "Remember, it is not the purpose of the Representative Man to be destructive to persons but to liberate them." Then they went on to another community.

As they continued their journey, someone said, "Lord, I will go with you anywhere." To that thoughtless promise Jesus responded, "Foxes have holes in which to sleep, and birds have nests in which to rest, but the Representative Man has no earthly home." Then Jesus invited another, "Come along with me, anyway." Hesitating, the man said, "Lord, wait until my father dies and is buried. Then I will." Jesus said, "Let those who are spiritually dead conduct the funerals of those who die physically. As for you, go and proclaim the Spirit dimension." Still another responded, "Lord, I want to accompany you. Let me first say goodbye to my family and friends." Jesus instructed that person, "Anyone who makes a sincere commitment to me and then entangles himself in his old relationships disqualifies himself for participation in the Spirit dimension."

MAKE YOUR JOURNEY SIMPLE

After this, Jesus commissioned seventy other persons to travel together in twos as advance teams. They made a preparatory call on every city and town he intended to visit on the way to Jerusalem. Before he sent them out, he instructed them: "The work in which we are engaged is like a harvest that is mature and very large. There are not many helpers, so ask God to provide additional helpers to gather the harvest. As you go to these various cities before my arrival, be aware that you are like lambs in the midst of angry wolves. Don't carry a wallet or bag or shoes. Don't stop to pass the time of day along the way. When you are invited into a house, go in and say right off, 'God bless your house.' If the presence of God is already in that house, your blessing will be effective, but if not, it will return to you. To whatever house you are invited, stay there, accepting whatever food and hospitality they offer. Don't feel bad about taking it, because just like the worker in the field, you are worth what you get. Don't be shifting from one house to another. Don't be ill mannered, but when you are received into a house, appreciate whatever is given you. Demonstrate the truth you speak by making the sick well and telling them, 'The Spirit dimension has burst forth among you.' Whenever you meet rejection in a town, walk on down the street and say to them, 'We are taking nothing from your city, not even the dust off your street, but you should be fully aware that the Spirit dimension has burst forth among you.'"

LUKE 9:51–10:11

CELEBRATE THE
FULFILLMENT THAT IS YOURS

Later on, these seventy came back ecstatic with joy. They said, "Lord, even those alien spirits respond to us when we use the power of your name." He said to them, "Yes, I saw those alien spirits fall from heaven. Indeed, I give you authority over every form through which the Adversary works, and no expression of his power will hurt you. But don't celebrate your power over the spirits. Rather, celebrate the fact that you have a relationship with God."

LUKE 10:17–20

One time when they were alone, he said to his understudies, "You are certainly fulfilled by experiencing the things you have seen and heard. Do you realize that many of God's spokespersons, even the rulers of the world, have wanted to experience these things but haven't? They wanted to hear the sayings you have heard, but they didn't."

DAY 36

AUTHENTIC LIFE

On another occasion, an enforcer of the rules got Jesus' attention and tried to trap him: "Teacher, what must I do to have authentic life age after age?" Jesus responded to him in terms he understood, asking, "What do the rules say? How do you interpret them?" Immediately the man answered, "'You are to love God with all of your feelings, with all of your inner being, with all of your power, with all of your intelligence.' And also, 'You are to love every other person as you love yourself.'" Then Jesus instructed him, "You have offered a very good answer. Practice it, and you will have authentic life." But this enforcer of the rules, seeking to escape responsibility for his life, asked Jesus, "Who is meant by 'every other person'?"

In response, Jesus told this story: "A man who was making a trip from Jerusalem down to Jericho was held up and attacked on the way. His attackers stripped off his clothes, beat him, and left him nearly dead. After a while, a religious leader came by, and when he saw the suffering man, he very carefully avoided any contact with him. The same thing happened when an assistant to the leader passed that way. When he saw the wounded man, he, too, avoided contact with him. Then along came a foreigner, and when he saw what had happened, he had deep feelings of compassion. He rushed over, treated the man's wounds, and bandaged them carefully. He then transported him to the nearest inn, where he continued to care for him. The next day, when the foreigner was ready to depart, he gave money to the innkeeper with these instructions: 'You take care of this man, and whatever the bill comes to, I will pay you on my next trip.'

"Tell me, which of these three do you think really loved this man who was robbed and beaten?" asked Jesus. "The one who responded with care and concern for his needs," said the enforcer of the rules. Jesus said to him, "Right. You go and respond in like fashion to the needs of every person."

LUKE 10:23–37

WHERE TO GET STRENGTH

Once, after Jesus had finished praying, one of his understudies made this request: "Lord, instruct us in prayer just as John taught his disciples." He said to them, "Here is a way for you to pray: 'Father, we reverence your name. May the Spirit dimension expand to its ultimate fulfillment. Enable us to get the physical necessities for our lives each day. Continually forgive our failures, even as we forgive the failures of others. Lead us by your hand, and do not test us.'"

Jesus continued his teaching on prayer: "Suppose one of you goes to your neighbor about midnight to ask a favor—'Neighbor, let me borrow three loaves of bread. I have a friend who has stopped by to visit, but I have no food to offer.' Then suppose your neighbor responds, 'Don't bother me. I have already locked the door and put my children to bed. I can't get up and give you bread.' You know, even though the neighbor won't get up and give you bread because of your relationship, because you keep asking, your neighbor will get up and give you as much bread as you need."

LUKE 11:1–8

While Jesus was teaching, a woman in the crowd got his attention when she said, "How fulfilled is the woman who gave birth to you and nurtured you through her breasts." He responded, "That may be, but truly fulfilled are those who hear God's message and respond to it."

LUKE 11:27–28

DAY 37

LIFE IS MORE THAN POSSESSIONS

When Jesus had finished his sayings, a man standing in the crowd shouted to him, "Teacher, speak to my brother and make him share the inheritance with me." Jesus responded, "Man, do you think I am a judge or an arbitrator to settle your disputes?" This request inspired him to speak to the crowd about material possessions. "Examine your lives, and take note of your desire to possess more and more. A person does not fulfill his life by the accumulation of material possessions." To illustrate the point, he told this story: "A very wealthy farmer continued to have one bumper crop after another. He began musing to himself, 'What will I do with these vast harvests I am producing? Where will I store them, because my barns are already full.' Then he said, 'I know what I can do. I'll tear down my old barns and I will build larger barns. Then I will have plenty of room to store my crops. With all these possessions, I will say to myself, "You are secure.

You have stored enough possessions to last your whole life. Take it easy. Eat what you want, drink what you want, celebrate life.'" God said to this man, 'You're a very foolish person, and you have adopted false values. Tonight you will die. When you die, who will own all the things you have amassed?' And that's how it is when a person has inverted his values, gaining the wealth of material possessions without gaining the wealth of a relationship with God.

LUKE 12:13–21

"Be ready for whatever comes, dressed for action, with your lights on. Live like persons who are awaiting their employer's return from his wedding. Whenever he returns and knocks at the door, be awake so that you may invite him in at once. How fulfilled are those employees whom the employer will find awake when he returns! I may shock you when I tell you that he will change his clothes and invite them to sit down for a meal and serve them himself. Keep watching for him, even if he comes late at night or early in the morning; watch for his return, because you will truly be fulfilled if you stay alert. Take the analogy of a good man whose house was broken into. If he had known when the robber would break into his house, he would have stayed awake and protected his property. I'm telling you to stay awake, because the representative Man will come to you when you are not expecting him."

BE RESPONSIBLE FOR YOUR LIFE

At these words, Peter asked him, "Lord, are you telling this story for our benefit or for the benefit of everyone here?" Jesus responded, "Who will be that responsible manager to whom the owner can delegate responsibility for his family, to feed them at the proper time? The person will be truly fulfilled whom the owner finds doing this at the time of his arrival. It will be this person to whom the owner gives complete authority and responsibility for everything he owns. If, during the time he is waiting, that employee says to himself, 'My employer has been gone a long time,' and begins to mistreat the men and women who report to him and spends his hours eating and drinking and getting drunk, that person's employer will come back to examine the business when he is not expecting it at all. The employer will fire the manager and kick him out into the streets to join the ranks of the unemployed. The person who has clear knowledge of what he ought to be doing and doesn't do it will suffer severe consequences for his indolence. But the person who is unclear in his responsibility, even when he fails, will receive consideration because of his ignorance. The person who has been given great knowledge and insight is expected to live according to it. You yourself expect a great deal more from persons who are given greater responsibility."

LUKE 12:35–48

DAY 38

DON'T MISS YOUR LIFE'S MEANING

At this time in Jesus' ministry, some persons reported to him how Pilate had killed a group of Galileans and mixed their blood with pagan sacrifices. Jesus shocked those who reported the incident by asking, "Do you think that these Galileans were worse persons than the other citizens of that region because this happened to them? Well, I can tell you they were not, and unless you change your attitude and your behavior, you will die without experiencing the meaning of your lives. Do you remember the eighteen persons who were crushed when the tower in Siloam fell on them? Do you think they were worse than others living in Jerusalem? Well, I can tell you they were not, and unless you change your attitude and your behavior, you will die without experiencing the meaning of your lives."

Then Jesus told this story: "Once there was a man who planted a fig tree in his vineyard. One day he came out looking for figs but couldn't find any. He said to the man who pruned his vines, 'Look here, for three years I have been expecting this tree to bear fruit, and it hasn't borne any yet. Cut it down—why is it taking up space?' And the man who pruned his vineyard said, 'Sir, give it one more year. Let me dig around it and fertilize it. If it bears fruit next year, that will be good. If not, I'll cut it down.'"

PERSONS AND CULTURAL MORES

Jesus went to teach in one of the religious meetings that the Jewish people had on their sacred day. While he was in the meetinghouse, a woman came in who had suffered an affliction for eighteen years. She was bent over and couldn't straighten herself. Jesus scanned the crowd and spotted her. He then called out to her, "Woman, you are freed from your affliction." She came over, and he laid his hands on her. At once she stood up straight and praised and worshiped God. But the man who was in charge of the meeting was filled with hostility because Jesus had made this woman whole on the sacred day: "We have six days in which to do our work. Persons should be healed on one of those days and not on our sacred day." Jesus responded, "You phony! Does not each of you untie your ox or ass and lead it from the

-103-

stall to water on the rest day? If you treat your animals with compassion, why shouldn't this woman be liberated from her affliction on the sacred day? She shares in the promise God made to Abraham, and yet the Adversary has bound her up for eighteen years." This argument both embarrassed and silenced his opposition. Everyone present began celebrating the marvelous things they had seen him do.

LUKE 13:1–17

And Jesus went through the towns and villages teaching about the Spirit dimension as he made his way toward Jerusalem. Someone in the crowd asked him, "Sir, is it for just a few people to discover the meaning of their lives?" He responded, "Be disciplined in your efforts. Many persons will give it a try but will not succeed. At some point, the door of opportunity will be closed and locked. After that, many will stand outside crying, 'Sir, sir, open the door of opportunity to us again.' But the man in the house will respond, 'I don't know who you are.' Those standing outside will argue, 'We have had meals with you; we have sipped wine with you; and you taught us in the streets of our villages.' But again he will refuse them, saying, 'I don't know you. Go away. You have wasted your lives.' You will be filled with grief and remorse when you recognize Abraham, Isaac, and Jacob and all of God's spokespersons participating in the Spirit dimension's fulfillment and find yourselves excluded from it. Persons will come from all over the world, from east and west, from north and south, to participate in the Spirit dimension. Now listen to this—some who are last to participate will be highly esteemed, and those who first had the opportunity will be the last to share in the fulfillment."

RESPOND WHILE YOU CAN

The same day he was making these pronouncements, several representatives from the rule keepers said to him, "You had better get out of the country, because Herod is going to kill you." Jesus responded, "Go tell that cunning old man what I have to say. Look, I am getting rid of negative forces and unifying people, and I am healing people today and tomorrow, and the third day I will be fulfilled. Whatever lies before me, I will continue today, tomorrow, and the day afterward. No spokesperson for God will die outside Jerusalem. O, Jerusalem, you have killed God's spokespersons; you have persecuted the ambassadors he sent to you. Many times I would have unified you and protected you, just as a hen does when she gathers her chicks under her wings, and you wouldn't let me. Look how empty you are! Look how deserted you are! You will not have another

-104-

opportunity to respond to me until that day comes when you will say, 'How marvelous is the person who comes to represent the Lord!'"

PERSONS OUTRANK RULES

On one occasion, Jesus went home to dinner with one of the prominent rule keepers. It was the sacred day, and those who opposed him observed his behavior very carefully. On the way to his house, they met a man who was sick. Jesus took this as an opportunity to engage the pious rule keepers and interpreters in a conversation. He asked, "Is it permitted to heal this person on the rest day?" Not one of them responded to his question, because they were hoping for an infraction of the rules on Jesus' part so that they could indict him. He then touched the man who was sick, made him whole, and sent him home. In his own defense, Jesus asked, "If one of your horses or cows should fall into a hole on the sacred day, wouldn't you immediately get it out?" Once again, they were silent.

DAY 39

LET OTHERS AFFIRM YOU

When they got to the home of the prominent rule keeper, Jesus noted how the guests selected their seats. He told them this story, which contradicted their practices: "When someone invites you to a dinner party, don't choose the most prominent seats, because someone who deserves those seats may arrive late. If you have chosen the best seats, it may create an embarrassing situation for you and the host when the host says to you, 'Will you give this guest your seat and take one less prominent?' When you are invited to a dinner, take a less conspicuous seat and then the host can say to you, 'My dear friend, I want you to be sitting closer to me. Sit here in this prominent place.' Then those other guests who are invited to the reception will recognize the intimate relationship that you have with the host. Those who choose the most prominent positions for themselves incur jealousy and humiliation and, finally, rejection. But those persons who do not demand the best for themselves often have it given to them."

BE INCLUSIVE IN YOUR RELATIONS

Then, turning to the pious rule keeper who had invited him to dinner, he said, "Whenever you have a celebration like this, take care how you formulate the guest list. Don't just invite friends, fellow rule keepers, your relatives, and your rich neighbors—because all these persons can return your invitation. When you have a dinner party, invite the poor, the crippled, the deformed, and the blind. When you include these social outcasts, you will really be fulfilled. You see, they can't pay you back now, but you will be rewarded at the ultimate fulfillment."

While they were sitting around the table after Jesus had given this directive, one of his fellow guests said, "How fulfilled is the person who is invited to celebrate the ultimate fulfillment of the Spirit dimension!" That statement moved Jesus to tell another story: "Once upon a time, a man prepared a large dinner party and invited a long list of friends to celebrate with him. When the dinner was prepared, he sent one of his employees to tell all his friends that the dinner was ready. The courier said, 'Come to the party, for everything is now prepared.' Every person who had been invited offered reasons why he or she could not come. The first invitee said, 'I have purchased a farm, and I need to go and look at it. Please accept my regrets.' A second person said, 'I have purchased five pairs of oxen with which to work my land, and I need to test them. Please accept my regrets.' And still another guest responded, 'I have recently married and I just cannot come.' Then the courier reported to his employer what all these guests had said. Their responses made the host really angry, and he said to the courier, 'Go out right now and invite everybody you meet on the streets and in the alleys to come to the party. Invite the poor, the deformed, the lame, and the blind.' 'Sir, it's done just as you have requested, and there is still more food than they can eat,' responded the courier. Then the host instructed him, 'Go out into the countryside and make every person in sight come, so my house can be filled. But I'll tell you one thing: not a single one of those persons who were originally asked will taste the food.'"

PLAN YOUR LIFE RESPONSIBLY

On another occasion, a large crowd of people was following Jesus, and he paused to give them these instructions: "All who meet and desire to accompany me must give the relation priority over their father, mother, wife, children, brothers, sisters, and their own safety. Unless they do, they cannot be my intimate companions. And whoever does not take responsibility for his own life and experience his fulfillment in relationship with me cannot be my understudy.

"If you wanted to build a tower so that you could see your enemy approaching, wouldn't you first calculate the cost of the materials and the labor to erect it, to determine whether or not you were able to build it? You would plan carefully, because if you laid the foundation and built it perfectly but that's as far as you got, everyone who saw the half-finished tower would laugh at you. Many would say, 'Look at that half-finished tower! That man made a good start, but he wasn't able to complete it.' A ruler intending to attack another nation very carefully considers whether or not he has the soldiers and the weapons to win a victory. If he doesn't accurately assess his possibilities, he may have to negotiate a peace before the first battle. Calculate the cost of being my understudy. It means giving up everything you have."

LUKE 13:22–14:33

DAY 40

EVERYONE IS IMPORTANT

On another occasion, a large number of tax collectors and outcasts gathered around listening to Jesus. Observing this, the rule keepers and the interpreters of the rules began griping, "Why, this man courts the friendship of outcasts and goes out for meals with them."

Then Jesus told them this story to benefit them: "If you had a hundred sheep grazing in the pasture and one of them got lost, wouldn't you leave the ninety-nine by themselves and go search for the lost sheep until you found it? And when you found it, would you not place it on your shoulders and come home celebrating? And when you got home, you would call your friends and neighbors and say to them, 'Celebrate with me, because I have found my one lost sheep.' I want you to know that there is more celebration in the presence of God over one outcast who changes his attitude and behavior than over ninety-nine persons whose attitude and behavior remain fixed.

"If a woman has ten silver pieces and loses one of them, won't she turn on every light in the house and sweep it from wall to wall until she finds the piece she has lost? When at last she has found the silver piece, she will say to her friends and neighbors, 'Celebrate with me, because I have found the silver piece I lost.' Well, I want you to know there is a celebration in the presence of God when one outcast changes his attitude and behavior."

Jesus continued with another story: "Once upon a time, a man had two sons. The younger said to his father, 'Dad, give me my inheritance now,' and the father did so. A few days after he received his inheritance, the younger son gathered his wealth and took a trip far away from home and spent his inheritance in undisciplined living. About the time his money ran out, the country to which he had gone was in a great depression, and he became hungry and cold. He went to a landowner and asked him for work. That man sent him into his fields to feed hogs. The young man was so hungry, he would have eaten what the hogs left, and still no one gave him anything to eat. Then he came to his true self and said, 'Why, even my father's hired hands have more than enough to eat, while I am starving! I will go home to my father and confess, "Father, I have failed you. I feel unworthy to be called your son, so I beg you to let me be your employee."' Leaving behind the hogs, the pasture, and the foreign country, he went home. Before he got near the house, while he was yet at a distance, his father saw him coming. His father had such a deep feeling of love and forgiveness that he uncharacteristically ran out to meet his son, to hug and kiss him. His son began to confess, 'I have failed God, I have failed you, and I have failed myself. I am unworthy to be your child.'

"Paying no attention to his words, the father said to his employees, 'Bring my son the best clothes we have; give him a pair of shoes; and put the family ring on his hand, signifying his complete acceptance. Butcher the beef; prepare a feast, and make ready a celebration. My son was as good as dead and is alive again. He has been lost, and now he has found the way home.' And the celebration began.

"At the time of the younger son's arrival, the older brother was working in the field. When he got within earshot of the house, he heard the music and the dancing. He called one of the employees over to him and asked, 'What's going on here?' The employee answered, 'Your brother has come back home, and your father has prepared a banquet to celebrate his arrival.'

"That news so angered the older brother that he wouldn't participate in the celebration. When his father heard about it, he came out and tried to persuade the older son to come in to the party. The older brother declared, 'All these years, I've done what you have asked me to do. At no time have I disobeyed you, and you never so much as killed a goat for me to celebrate with my friends. But just as soon as your rebellious son, who has wasted his inheritance with high living and loose women, comes home, you butcher for him the beef we have spent months fattening.'

"His father replied, 'My dear son, you have been with me every day, and everything I have belongs to you. It is proper for us to celebrate and to be joyous, because your brother was as good as dead, and now he is alive. He was confused and lost, and now he has discovered the way home."

DAY 41

MANAGE YOUR LIFE RESPONSIBLY

Jesus then spoke again with his understudies about the power of material possessions. He said, "Once there was a very wealthy man who had a manager.

Someone accused the manager of being wasteful. The man of wealth demanded a conference and asked, 'Why am I getting these reports? Give me an accounting of your management. Until these accusations are cleared, you cannot go on managing.' The manager, being dishonest, began to plot for his own benefit. 'What can I do?' he asked himself. 'My boss is going to fire me, and I can't work with my hands, and I am ashamed to ask anyone to give me money. I know what I can do!' he thought to himself. 'I will create obligations with my boss's debtors so that when I am fired, I will have friends to look after me.' He called in one of the debtors. 'How much do you owe my boss?' he asked. The man answered, 'One hundred barrels of oil.' He said, 'Take this bill and quickly write on it that you owe him fifty.' Then he said to another debtor, 'How much do you owe?' and that one replied, 'One hundred bushels of wheat.' The manager said to him, 'Take your bill and write 'eighty bushels.'"

"Strange as it may seem, this man's boss recognized that his manager had provided for his own needs. You will recognize that persons living in tune with the values of this age take better care of themselves than persons living for the future. Here's my point: Cultivate a group of friends who know how to make money and get along in this world so that if you come up lacking, they can help you out.

"Trustworthy management has little to do with the size of the task. A person trustworthy with a small responsibility will be just as trustworthy with a larger one. Likewise, a person who is irresponsible in a small task will be just as irresponsible with a large one. If you don't learn to manage your money and meet your obligations, how can you be trusted with the wealth of spiritual values? Also, if you don't know how to manage well what belongs to another person, how do you ever hope to have anything of your own to manage? No person can live with competing values. That would be self-destructive schizophrenia. When a person finds himself in contradictory circumstances, he must choose one and reject the other. He must devote himself to one to the neglect of the other. You simply cannot live with double loyalties—one to God and the other to money."

LUKE 15:1–16:15

GREED BREEDS INSENSITIVITY

"Once there was a very wealthy man who dressed well and lived high. Sitting at his property gate was a beggar named Lazarus, a filthy man covered with sores. All he wanted were the scraps that were left over from the meals at the rich man's house. What's more, the neighborhood dogs came by and licked his sores. One day, this beggar died and went into the presence of

God. The wealthy man, too, died and was buried. Through the anguish and pain consequent to his greed, he became aware of God, and suddenly Lazarus appeared. The wealthy man screamed, 'Oh, God, help me! Let Lazarus come and help me! Just let him dip his finger in water and drip it on my tongue to ease the pain I am feeling!'

"God answered, 'Don't you remember how it was with you during your life? You had everything you wanted, and Lazarus had nothing. Now the reverse is true. He is fulfilled, and you are experiencing meaninglessness and despair. In addition, there is a huge chasm without a passage between us and you.'

"'Do me one favor,' the wealthy man requested. 'Send Lazarus to my family to warn them. You see, I have five brothers, and I want them to know what is really important in life, lest they wind up in meaningless pain and despair.' God said, 'They have the rules and the records of my spokespersons. Let them respond to their message.' 'Oh, no,' the wealthy man said, 'they won't listen to that any more than I did, but if someone returned from death to instruct them, they would change their attitude and behavior.' But God said to the suffering man, 'If they don't respond to the rules and the explanations made by my spokespersons, they will not be convinced by someone rising from among the dead.'

LUKE 16:19–31

"If you have an employee working under you, plowing your field or feeding your livestock, when he comes in from work, you don't say, 'Go, sit down and eat.' Rather, you instruct him, 'Prepare my food, please. Put on an apron, and set my food on the table. When I have finished eating and drinking, then you can eat and drink.' When you have finished eating, do you feel a great sense of gratitude because your employee has done what you asked him? Certainly not. And that's how it is with you, when you have done the things that you ought to do. You might say, 'We haven't shown any special qualities as employees. We have simply done our duty.'"

BE GRATEFUL FOR GOD'S GIFTS

When Jesus was going up to Jerusalem, he went through the region between Samaria and Galilee. As he came into one of the villages, ten leprous men came out to meet him, but they stood at a distance. In unison they cried out, "Jesus, Teacher, be kind to us!" As soon as he was aware of their request, he told them, "Go, let your religious officials examine you in compliance with the rules." And as soon as they started on their way, they were healed of their leprosy. Only one of them, however, shouted aloud, "Praise God!" when he recognized that he had been cured. This one man returned to Jesus and knelt down before him, and it so happened that this man was a Samaritan. Jesus asked him, "Weren't there ten of you? Where are the other nine?" But only this one foreigner had come back to give thanks to God and to offer praise. Jesus said to him, "Get up and go on to the religious officials for your examination. Your trust has made you whole."

DAY 41

HOW THE SPIRIT
DIMENSION MANIFESTS ITSELF

On another occasion, the rule keepers queried Jesus about the objective appearance of the Spirit dimension. He answered, "The Spirit dimension will not appear with a great fanfare; nor will you hear couriers saying, 'Here it is!' You must understand this: the Spirit dimension is inside you." He turned to his understudies and said, "The time will come when you will long for the fulfillment that the Representative Man will eventually bring, and it won't come. Deceivers will say, 'Look, he's coming here,' or 'Let's go there to meet him there,' but don't pay them any attention. The reappearance of the Representative Man will be as sudden as lightning flashing from one side of the sky to the other. Before that day comes, he must experience the pain and rejection of this generation of people. The day in which the Representative Man appears will be something like the days in which Noah lived. All the people were eating and drinking, making merry and celebrating, until Noah entered his large boat. Then a flood came, and everyone drowned. You recall that Lot had a similar experience. The people around him ate and drank. They conducted their business and constructed buildings. But the very day that Lot departed from Sodom, the city and all its inhabitants were destroyed. It will be like that when the Representative Man returns. On the day of his return, each person must respond from where he is. If you are on the top of the house, don't go inside to get your belongings. If you are in the field, don't even turn back to the house. Recall how Lot's wife turned into a pillar of salt when she turned back. All who try to preserve their lives will give them up, but all who give up their lives voluntarily will actually keep them. When the day of return finally arrives, two persons will be sleeping in one bed; one of them will be taken, and the other will be left. Two women will be working together, and one of them will depart while the other stays."

His understudies asked, "Where will all this take place, Lord?" and he said to them, "As surely as eagles gather to feed where the carcass is, so will the time of judgment come when and where God chooses."

PERSIST IN PRAYER

Then Jesus told a story about how persons should continue in prayer and not be discouraged when an answer is delayed: "Once there was a judge in a certain city who had no regard either for God or for persons. In that same city, there was a widow who petitioned the judge, 'Make right this wrong that has been done to me.' And for a long time, the judge wouldn't do anything about it. But finally he thought to himself, 'Even though I don't respect God or persons, because this woman is continually nagging me with her requests, I will do what she wants, to silence her.'"

Then Jesus said, "Pay attention to what this insensitive judge said. If the judge granted the woman's request, don't you believe God will respond to the people who constantly pray? Will he wait a long time to answer them? I assure you that he will respond, and when he does, it will be quick and deliberate. But I wonder, when the Representative Man returns, will there be anyone who trusts God?"

RECOGNIZE YOUR UNITY WITH OTHER PERSONS

Jesus then told this story about persons who consider themselves better than other people and even look down on others: "Once upon a time, two men went into the house of God to worship. One of these was a pious rule keeper, and the other was a tax collector. Here's how the rule keeper prayed: 'God, I thank you that I am better than other people. For example, I'm better than those who make excessive profits, who are crooked in their dealings, who are unfaithful to their wives. I am better than that tax collector over there. To demonstrate my commitment to you, I do without food two times every week, and I give 10 percent of everything I make to charity.'

"The tax collector who was standing in the corner wouldn't even look up to God but sank his chin into his chest, muttering, 'God, be kind to me because I am off the track.' This man, not the rule keeper, went home with a right relationship to God. Every person who pumps up a false self-image will be deflated, and the person who honestly practices self-acceptance before God will be changed by God's love."

LUKE 17:7–18:14

GOD'S PURPOSE IN MARRIAGE

When Jesus had finished talking to his followers about forgiveness, he left Galilee and went back into Judea, which is on the other side of the Jordan River. Great crowds continued to follow him, and he regularly healed those who were afflicted. Back in Judea, a group of the rule keepers began interrogating him: "Can a man get a divorce for any reason he desires?" Jesus replied, "Don't you know what the record says? In the very beginning, the Creator made human beings male and female. In the basic structure of creation, it is designed for a man to separate himself from his father and his mother and to be joined to his wife. Their union will create a new unit of society. After they are married, they are no longer two separate individuals but constitute a new unity. When God so joins two persons, nobody should separate them."

"Well," they said, "why did Moses say that if a man wishes a divorce, let him put it in writing, give it to his wife, and send her on her way?" Jesus explained, "Because of your insensitivity to each other and the destructiveness of your relationships, Moses instructed you how to terminate a marriage, but that is not in accordance with God's original purpose. I tell you, whoever sends his wife away without evidence that the relationship is already broken and dead, and then marries another woman, commits adultery."

His understudies were stunned by this statement. "If what you're saying is so, it seems to us that it would be better for a man never to marry." Jesus acknowledged, "Not everyone can accept the challenge I am about to offer. There are different reasons for a person's not having an active sex life. By birth, some persons may have no sexual desire. Others may be castrated, and still others may sublimate their sexual desire through their work for God. If you can accept this challenge, do so."

On another occasion, some eager parents brought their little children to Jesus, hoping that he would lay his hands on them and pray over them. Some of his understudies chided the parents and told them to go away. But Jesus said, "Don't put down the good intentions of these parents. Encourage them to bring their children to me, because the children symbolize the Spirit dimension." And Jesus gently placed his hands on the children. When he had finished praying for them, he left.

DAY 42

THE DANGER OF WEALTH

One day, a young man ran up to Jesus and asked, "Good teacher, what must I do to live forever?" Jesus answered, "First of all, why do you describe me as 'good'? God is the only truly good one. But in response to your question, if you really want to live, keep the rules." "Which ones?" the young man wanted to know. Jesus said, "You shall not destroy another person; you shall not have sex with anyone but your wife when you marry; you shall not take what belongs to somebody else; you shall not lie about another; respect your parents; and you must love every other person as you love yourself." Quite confidently, the young man responded, "I've been doing all these ever since I was a child. What is still missing?" Then Jesus directed, "If you really want to be complete, sell all your possessions and distribute the money to those who don't have any. That will enable you to reorder your values. Then follow me, and you will experience authentic life." When the young man heard Jesus' explanation, he was depressed and turned and walked slowly away, for he was extremely wealthy.

As Jesus watched him walk away, he turned to his understudies and said, "I am giving you a clear message when I say that a wealthy person will have great difficulty entering the Spirit dimension. It is much easier for a camel to get on its knees and crawl through the low gate in the wall of the city than for a wealthy person to give himself unreservedly to God's purpose." When his understudies heard this statement, they were so shocked that they asked Jesus, "Who, then, can be made whole?" When Jesus saw their consternation, he said, "True wholeness cannot be achieved by a person in his own strength, but anything and everything is possible with God."

THE UNDERSTUDIES' REWARD

Peter reflected on what Jesus had said and raised this question: "Look, we have given up everything to be with you and to understand your message. Now, what will we get out of it?" Jesus responded, "Honestly, in the re-creation of all things, when the Representative Man exercises both power and authority, you, too, will have power and authority guiding and directing the twelve tribes of Israel. Not only you, but everyone who leaves his home or brothers or sisters or parents or wife or children or possessions of any kind for me will get it all back a hundred times over during this life, and then he will truly have deathless life—the life of the ages. But remember this: many who are prominent and powerful in this life will go unnoticed in the next. And many who are powerless and poor today will rule in the life to come.

GOD'S WAY IS NOT THE HUMAN WAY

"Life in the Spirit dimension may also be compared to a manager of laborers. At six o'clock one morning, the manager arrived at the labor pool to hire workers for the vineyard. After he had negotiated an acceptable day's wage, he put them to work. Again, at about nine o'clock, he walked by the labor pool and saw several men standing idle. He said to them, 'If you will put in the rest of the day working in my vineyard, I will pay you an appropriate wage.' So they went to work. He also went down to the labor pool at about noon and again at three o'clock in the afternoon, and he did as he had previously done. Then, at five o'clock, he went past the labor pool and found still others who were idle. He said to them, 'Why have you not been working today?' 'Because no one has given us a job,' they replied. He said, 'Go and finish out the day working at my vineyard, and I will give you whatever is appropriate.'

"At six, the manager said to the treasurer of the company, 'Call all the workers together and pay them off, beginning with those I hired last.' And those who were hired at five o'clock and had worked only one hour were paid the same wage as those who had worked all day. When those who had worked all day came to receive their checks, they naturally felt that they deserved more than those who had worked only one hour, but they received the same thing. When they looked at their checks, they began complaining about the manager's injustice. They reasoned, 'These men who worked one hour have been paid the same as those of us who worked not only longer but during the heat of the day.' The manager responded, 'Good fellows, didn't you receive the agreed-upon wage? Take what you have earned and go on home. I will pay these who worked but one hour the same that I paid you. Can't I do with my resources whatever I please? If I choose to be generous with these who have as great a need as you, why do you call my generosity evil?'" Jesus explained, "Many who enter the Spirit dimension late will actually have priority, and those who originally had priority will lose it."

MATTHEW 19:1–20:16

DAY 43

JOURNEY TO FULFILLMENT

One day, as the understudies were traveling along the road to Jerusalem with Jesus, they had an awesome experience that shattered their consciousness and left them frightened. This occurred when Jesus told them what was about to happen to him. He explained, "We are on the way to Jerusalem, where the Representative Man will be handed over to the religious leaders and the interpreters of the rules, and they will sentence him to die. They will then hand him over to the non-Jews, who will abuse him in every way imaginable—verbally, mentally, and physically—and they will kill him, and on the third day he will experience resurrection."

As they continued the trip, James and John, Zebedee's sons, came to Jesus with a request: "Teacher, give us the thing that we most deeply desire." "What is that?" Jesus queried. They answered, "We want to have places of importance when you begin wielding your power and authority." Jesus said, "You really don't understand me or the nature of my authority. Can you stand firm in your commitment as I do? Can you accept the consequences of your choices as I will?" And they said, "We can." Jesus responded, "You will indeed stick with your commitment, and you will also suffer the consequences of that decision. It is not my prerogative, however, to designate the seats of importance, because they have already been designated."

When the other understudies overheard what was being discussed, they were furious with James and John. Jesus gathered them all together and said, "You know that in the structures of power that the non-Jews have established, persons of prominence rule those of lesser importance, and the chain of command stretches from the highest to the lowest. That order of authority is not appropriate for you. If you want great importance, you must be one who ministers to the needs of others. If you want the highest position, you must serve every person. The Representative Man did not come to rule over persons but to serve them and to give himself to free them for what God intended."

MARK 10:32–45

JESUS RESTORES PERSONS

Jesus went on through the city of Jericho on his way to Jerusalem. A resident of Jericho named Zacchaeus, the leading tax collector and a very wealthy man, wanted to see Jesus. He tried hard but couldn't get a glimpse of Jesus because of both his own size and the size of the crowd. So Zac-

---

Jesus: Victim and Victor

After only three years of going about the countryside preaching, teaching, and helping many who suffered, Jesus was executed. The reason for the execution as set forth in the New Testament was a growing conflict developing between Jesus and the religious authorities—the high priest of the Jewish nation, the council, the rule keepers, and the materialists. The high priest gave both spiritual and political leadership to the nation of Israel; the council was composed of other officials who shared in major decision making; the rule keepers and the materialists were sects

(continued)

---

chaeus ran ahead, climbed a sycamore tree, and waited. When Jesus got to the base of the tree, he stopped, looked up, and spoke to him directly: "Hurry and come down, Zacchaeus, because I want to eat at your house today." Zacchaeus quickly slid down the tree, greeted Jesus, and escorted him to his house. When the crowd saw Jesus leave with him, they were stunned. "Why, he's going to have lunch with a man who is a social and moral outcast!"

During the course of their visit, Zacchaeus jumped to his feet and said, "Look, sir, I will give the poor half of everything I have, and for every one dollar of excess tax I have collected, I will return four." Jesus proclaimed, "Today, you and your whole family have been made whole because you are the offspring of Abraham. The Representative Man has come to seek out and restore those who have lost their sense of meaning and direction."

MANAGE YOUR RESOURCES WELL

By this time, they were getting near Jerusalem, and the crowd was anticipating the Spirit dimension would erupt with a revolutionary impact. So Jesus told this story: "Once upon a time, a ruler went into a distant country to have additional power and responsibility bestowed on him. Later, he returned to his own country. But before he left, he called together ten employees and gave each of them a hundred dollars with these instructions: 'Manage this until I return.' The people whom he governed resented him, and after his departure, they sent him this word: 'We will not be governed by a man like you.' Eventually he came back from the country where he had gone to receive additional power and responsibility. He summoned his employees to whom he had given the money to get an accounting. The first one reported, 'Sir, your hundred dollars gained a thousand additional dol-

---

in the Jewish religion, both of which had been confronted by Jesus and held resentment against him.

Each year the Jewish nation celebrated the festival of Passover, recalling God's deliverance of the Israelites when they were slaves in Egypt. At the time of this festival, Jesus went to Jerusalem with his band of followers. He rode into town on a donkey—a mock triumphal entry. He cast out from the temple merchants who had set up money-exchange booths for all the visitors. His casting out the money changers created a stir that pushed the Jewish authorities over the edge.

(continued)

lars.' He said, 'You have managed well, and because you have been diligent, I will make you manager of ten cities.' The second employee reported, 'Sir, your hundred dollars gained five hundred more dollars.' And to this one, he said, 'You will manage five cities.' Another reported, 'Sir, here's the hundred dollars you gave me. I carefully wrapped the money in this cloth to preserve it. Because you are such a tough administrator, I was afraid of what you would do. It seems you are able to pick up a profit where you haven't even made an investment and to gather a crop where you didn't sow any seed.' The ruler responded, 'I will use the very words you have spoken to evaluate your management. You are an inept and irresponsible manager. You knew that I was a tough administrator, making a profit where I didn't invest, reaping a harvest where I didn't sow any seed. Since you knew how tough I am, why didn't you put my money in the bank, so that at least I could receive interest?' Then he said to the manager who made five hundred dollars, 'Take the hundred dollars from him and give it to the manager who has a thousand dollars.' Some of the observers said, 'But sir, he already has a thousand dollars.' 'I am telling you,' the administrator said, 'that everyone who has accumulated more because of his wise management will have more given to him, and everyone who does not manage wisely will have taken away what he has. And also, those citizens who do not want me to govern them—execute them for treason.'"

LUKE 19:1–27

JESUS OPENS EYES

As Jesus and his understudies left Jericho, accompanied by a crowd, they approached a blind beggar sitting by the road, Bartimaeus, the son of Timaeus. When someone in the crowd told him that Jesus of Nazareth

---

While the leaders of Israel were developing their plot to capture Jesus, he prepared his own Passover with his band of followers. Before the meal began, Jesus took off his robe, wrapped his body with a towel, took a basin of water, and knelt before his followers to wash their feet. He washed and dried their feet, one after another, until he came to Peter, who said, "You will not do this to me."

Jesus responded, "If I do not wash your feet, you have no part in my work and rule." Then Peter wanted to be washed all over, but Jesus simply washed his feet. In this humble act of service, Jesus ministered to those who would betray him, deny him, and forsake him.

---

was passing by, he began to call out, "Jesus, son of David, please help me!" Numerous persons in the crowd told him to be quiet, but Bartimaeus shouted even louder: "Jesus, son of David, please help me!" Jesus stopped. He told the understudies to bring the blind man to him. They called out to the blind man, "Take courage. Come over here. He wants to see you." The blind man pulled off his wrap, got up, and made his way toward Jesus. Jesus asked, "What do you want me to do for you?" The blind man answered, "Sir, I want to be able to see." "Now fulfill your destiny," Jesus said. "Your trust has made you a whole person." At that instant, Bartimaeus began to see, and he followed Jesus, fulfilling his destiny.

MARK 10:46b–52

DAY 44

JESUS' LAST WEEK

About this time, the Jews began preparing for the Passover, the celebration that marked their exodus from Egypt. In preparation for this celebration, many persons left the countryside to take up residence in Jerusalem. As the crowd gathered, many of them looked for Jesus and spoke of him among themselves as they stood in God's house, asking, "Do you think he will come to the festival?" As part of their plot against him, the religious officials and the rule keepers had put out the word that if he was seen by anyone, it should be reported so that they could arrest him.

JESUS AFFIRMS A LOVING ACT

About six days before the Passover, Jesus came back to Bethany, the home of Lazarus, whom he had raised from the dead. Lazarus's family prepared dinner for Jesus. Martha busied herself getting the food ready, but Lazarus and some friends they had invited sat at the table talking with Jesus. While they were talking, Mary took a full bottle of very expensive perfume and poured it over Jesus' feet. She then knelt down and dried his feet with her hair. The whole house was filled with the aroma of the perfume.

JOHN 11:55–12:3

Martha, however, spent her time preparing food and entertaining the guests. She said, "Lord, doesn't it matter to you that my sister has left all the work to me? Tell her to get up and come help me." With tenderness and understanding Jesus said, "Martha, Martha, you're anxious and concerned about all your responsibilities. But actually, only one thing is really important. Mary has rightly ordered her priorities and will be able to keep what she is receiving for a long, long time."

LUKE 10:40–42

Meanwhile, Judas Iscariot (the understudy who would betray Jesus) asked angrily, "Can you tell me why this perfume was not sold for a hundred dollars to meet the needs of the poor?" He reacted with hostility to the anointing because he was a thief and wanted the money deposited in the treasury he controlled. He wasn't really concerned about the poor. Jesus rebuked him, saying, "Don't criticize what she has done, because she has prepared my body to be buried. There will always be an opportunity for you to assist the poor. They will always be around, but I won't always be here."

Many of the Jews in the neighborhood and beyond came to the gathering not only to see Jesus but also to get a firsthand glimpse of Lazarus, who had been raised from the dead. The top religious officials held another consultation to figure out how they could put Lazarus to death. As long as he was around, he presented tangible evidence of Jesus' power, so that many Jews came to trust Jesus.

JOHN 12:4–11

DAY 45

ENTRY INTO JERUSALEM

While Jesus and his followers were in Bethany, the crowd began gathering in Jerusalem for the festival. Jesus sent ahead two of his understudies with these instructions: "Go into the next town, and there you will find a tethered colt, which no one has ridden. Untie it, and bring it here. If anyone questions you, just say, 'Our leader needs this animal.'" Those he sent away left, and they found the colt just as Jesus had said.

As they were untying the colt, the owners asked them what they were doing. And they said, "Our leader needs this animal." They brought the colt to Jesus, and after spreading some of their clothes on its back, they helped Jesus get on the colt. As he rode along the road, people began to lay their clothes in his path. As he approached Jerusalem, where the road descends from the Mount of Olives, the whole crowd of his understudies began to cheer and shout praises to God for all the wonders they had seen him do, saying, "Celebrate this king who represents the Lord, our God! Peace in heaven and praise from on high!"

When they heard these shouts, some of the rule keepers in the crowd said to Jesus, "Teacher, tell your followers to shut up." Jesus answered them,

"If these followers were silenced, those stones lying on the hillside would clap their hands and shout."

When he drew near Jerusalem, he stood and looked at it for a long time and began to cry. In the midst of his tears, he spoke to the city: "If you had just known, if you had just known about this day and the peace and fulfillment that it could bring to you . . . but now you are blind to it. In the days that lie ahead, your enemies will surround you and hem you in, and you won't be able to escape. Those who attack you will raze your buildings and kill your children and not leave one foundation stone on another, because you did not recognize the time when God visited you."

LUKE 19:29b–44

Jesus' entry into Jerusalem with his entourage caused quite a stir, and the people kept saying to one another, "Who is this? Who is this?" And the crowd began to chant, "This is Jesus, this is Jesus, the prophet of Nazareth from Galilee." Jesus went to the temple, and when a number of crippled persons and persons with deformities learned that he was there, they came to him for help, and he made them whole. When the religious officials and the interpreters of the rules observed what Jesus was doing, and when they heard the little children running through the building crying, "Recognize and honor David's son! Recognize and honor David's son!" they felt threatened and angry. These leaders approached Jesus and asked, "Do you hear what these kids are saying?" Jesus responded, "I surely do, but haven't you read in your sacred records how God has said, 'Even the children and the nursing babies will offer perfectly acceptable worship'?"

MATTHEW 21:10–12a, 14–16

A large group of Greeks who had come to the festival cornered Philip, an understudy from Bethsaida in Galilee, and requested, "Sir, we would like to have an interview with Jesus." Philip shared their request with Andrew, and they went to Jesus with it. Jesus responded in symbols: "The time has come for the Representative Man to be completely fulfilled. Take the symbol of a grain of wheat as an example. You know that unless it is planted, it will remain one grain, but if it is planted and dies, it multiplies itself. He who clings to his life and defends it will lose it; but the person who releases his life and experiences it fully will have life now and life forever. Any person who is my companion must share in every aspect of my life. My companion will ultimately be where I am. Anyone who is a companion with me will be honored by my Father.

"I am deeply distressed in my heart. What shall I do? Will I say, 'Father, don't let me experience what is before me'? No, for this very moment, I have come into the world. I will say, 'Father, fulfill yourself.'" At that moment he heard God say, "I have already fulfilled myself in you, and I will fulfill myself even more completely through you." The crowd standing around him heard a noise, but they thought it was thunder. Others said, "One of God's special messengers spoke to him." Jesus explained, "This message from God is not for me primarily but for you. This is the moment of God's declaration about the world. At this moment the Adversary who has exercised great power in history will be overthrown. And when I am lifted up above the earth, I will gather all persons to me." This was a symbolic way of describing his death.

The crowd pressed him, saying, "We have always understood that the Messiah will stay with us forever. What do you mean, 'The Representative Man must be lifted up'? Who is this Representative Man you are referring to?" Jesus said, "For a little while longer, you will encounter the purpose of life, because that life is with you. Make your decisions and choose your directions while you can see clearly, lest darkness suddenly fall. A person traveling in the dark can't see the way ahead. You have the purpose of life revealed to you. Trust the person who has shown it to you, so that you yourselves may participate in it." After Jesus said these things, he left and hid from the crowd.

DAY 46

JESUS' PURPOSE IS FULFILLMENT, NOT CONDEMNATION

Although the crowd had seen Jesus do many marvelous deeds, they still didn't trust him. It was as Isaiah, God's spokesperson of old, said: "God, who has trusted our witness? Who has recognized your hand at work in human affairs?" Possibly the crowds couldn't trust him, because as Isaiah also said, "God has closed their eyes and made them insensitive to their feelings, so that they can't see with their eyes or feel with their hearts and thus change their attitudes and behavior and be made whole." These are the things Isaiah spoke when he envisioned God resplendent with light and spoke about him. Some persons of note in Israel, however, did trust Jesus, but they didn't acknowledge their faith because they feared the rule keepers would expel them from worship. These Jewish leaders chose acceptance of their fellow humans above the acceptance of God.

Jesus continued his powerful teachings: "Every person who trusts in me does not simply trust me but also trusts the one who commissioned me. Everyone who sees me sees the one who commissioned me. I am a light entering into history to illuminate its purpose and meaning, and everyone who trusts me will be delivered from meaninglessness and despair. Even though a person grasps my message and still doesn't trust me, I will not condemn him. I did not come to condemn persons but to liberate and fulfill them according to God's purpose. Those who close their lives to me and reject what I am saying will be accountable to God. Actually, on the day of ultimate fulfillment, the word I have spoken will measure each person. I have not imagined what I have spoken, but I have spoken what my Father, who commissioned me, told me. I am fully convinced that he has told me to speak about life, authentic life age after age. So whatever I'm saying to you is what the Father has said to me."

JOHN 12:20–50

When he returned to Jerusalem from Bethany the next morning, without having had any breakfast, he became hungry on the way to the city. In the distance he saw a fig tree growing along the roadside, but when he got to it, he found no fruit at all, only leaves. In frustration he declared, "You will never produce fruit!" Immediately, the fig tree began to wilt. His understudies watched in amazement and whispered to one another, "Look how quickly the fig tree is withering!" Building on the incident, Jesus said, "I emphasize to you that if you have faith and so see reality clearly, you will not only speak to fig trees that are barren, but you will have authority to command mountains. You will say to the mountain, 'Depart and slide into the sea,' and it will be done. And everything you ask the Father with utter trust will come to pass."

JESUS REBUKES THE RELIGIOUS LEADERS

Later on, when he was in the building that was dedicated to God, the religious officials and the decision makers for the nation challenged his teaching. "What right have you to interfere with our order of life? Who gave you the right to act as you do?" they asked. "Since you are interrogating me," Jesus replied, "I also will interrogate you. You answer my question, and I will answer yours. Tell me, was the baptism from John according to God's purpose, or was it John's own creation?" The leaders withdrew for a brief discussion. They said, "If we say it was according to the will of God, his next question will be, 'Why didn't you submit it?' But if we say it was John's own idea, think what the people will do to us, because they believe John was authentic." After their conference, they reported to Jesus, "We choose not to disclose the answer to your question." Jesus responded, "Well, I choose not to answer yours, either."

Then Jesus continued his dialogue with the religious leaders. "Tell me what you think of this story," he said. "There was a man who had two boys.

He said to the older, 'Son, I want you to work with me in the business today.' The boy answered, 'I don't want to.' But after he thought about it, he changed his mind and went to work with his father. After speaking to his older son, he came to the younger and made the same request of him. Without any hesitation, the younger son said, 'Yes, sir, I'll be glad to help you.' But he never showed up all day. Which of these two boys did what his father really wanted?" The pious rule keepers responded, "The first." Jesus affirmed their answer and pointed to a far-reaching principle: "The tax collectors and women who sell their bodies for money will participate in the Spirit dimension before you do. You see, when John appeared, telling you how to relate to God and to one another, you didn't trust what he was saying. But the tax collectors and the women who sell their bodies trusted him. And even after you had seen the results of his work, you didn't change your mind and trust what he taught.

THE ESTABLISHMENT'S POWER WILL END

"Let me tell you another story that emphasizes the same idea and expands on it. Once upon a time, there was a wealthy landowner who decided to plant a vineyard. After he fenced in the vineyard, he built a winery, and beside the winery he built a tower from which he could observe the farthest corner of the vineyard. He then leased the vineyard to managers and set out on a trip around the world. In the course of his journey, when he realized it was time for his vineyard to bear fruit, he dispatched employees to go to the managers and ask for a percentage of the profit. But the managers killed one of these employees and beat the other two mercilessly. Then the landowner sent several more employees, but the managers treated them just as badly as they had the first group. Finally, the vineyard owner had no one left to send but his only son. Thinking to himself, 'Surely these managers will respect my son,' he sent him to the vineyards. When the managers saw the son, however, they began to plot together, saying, 'Look, this boy will inherit the vineyard and all this land. Let's kill him. Then we can take over the land for ourselves.' So they apprehended the son, dragged him out of the vineyard, and murdered him. Now, when the landowner returns, what do you think he will do to those managers?"

They replied, "He will fire them and prosecute them to the limit. Then he will find other managers to take care of his property, someone who will give him his share of the vineyard when it is ripe." Jesus said, "You are professionals in the religious business, and you understand the teachings our fathers have given us. Did you ever notice this statement of the ancients: 'The large stone that the mason continued to cast aside, that very stone has been chosen as the cornerstone of the building—that choice is so astounding, it must be God's own action'? Here is the point of my story: the supervision of God's work in the world will be taken away from you and will be given to others, who will return its increase to God." When the religious officials and the rule keepers heard all these stories, it became obvious that Jesus was describing them and their attitude toward him. They wanted to arrest him and put him in jail, but they feared the anger of the crowd, because the crowd was more and more convinced that he was the authentic spokesperson of God.

MATTHEW 21:18–46

DAY 47

JESUS AVOIDS ENTRAPMENT

After Jesus had told this story, the pious rule keepers held a caucus to discuss how they could force Jesus into a contradiction. When he had finished speaking, they sent representatives from their group, along with some representatives from the supporters of Herod, saying, "Teacher, we know that you are an authentic person, and you are teaching faithfully the ways of God. You don't care what people think about you, nor do you set one person above another. Being certain of your truthfulness, give us your opinion. Is it proper for us to pay tax to the Roman government or not?" Jesus was listening not only to their words but to the intent of their questioning, and he responded, "Why are you trying to trap me, you phonies? Give me a piece of the money with which you have been paying taxes." They handed him a silver coin. He asked, "Whose image is stamped on this coin? And whose inscription is written around its edges?" They answered him, "The Roman emperor and his inscription." Jesus replied, "Give to the Roman emperor the things that belong to him, and give to God the things that belong to God." The simplicity and directness of his answer struck them so forcefully that they gave up trying to trap him.

GOD IS GOD OF THE LIVING

No sooner had he answered the tax question then some of the religious aristocrats, who did not believe in resurrection, came to him. They asked him, "Teacher, you are familiar with the rules Moses handed down. He said, 'If a man marries and dies before he has any children, his brother ought to marry his wife and have children for the sake of his brother who died prematurely.' We have a case in point where there were seven brothers. The first one married, died prematurely, and having no children, his brother married his widow. This brother died, then the third and the fourth, and so on until all seven had married this woman. Finally, the woman died. Now, at resurrection, whose wife will this woman be, since each of these men married her and was properly joined to her?" Refusing to be caught in their trap, Jesus said, "Your problem is essentially your lack of understanding of what God has taught you and of the power that God has. In that form of existence beyond resurrection, persons will neither marry nor establish families but rather will be in the immediate family of God, just like as those who are now in his presence. With regard to the reality of resurrection, do you not know what God himself has said? 'I am God of Abraham, and God of Isaac, and God of Jacob. God is not God of nothing but of something, God not of nonbeing but of true being.'" When the crowd heard this response, a shocked hush fell over them.

MATTHEW 22:15–33

RULES FOR LIVING

One of the interpreters of the rules felt the impact of Jesus' answers to the ruling aristocrats, and he posed a question to Jesus: "What is the most important rule for living?" Immediately Jesus responded, "The most important rule is, 'Listen, Israel, the Lord our God is one; and you are to love the Lord your God with all your feelings, with all your inner being, and with all your intelligence to the fullest of your capacity.' This is the most important rule. Next in importance is the rule to 'love every person just as you love yourself.' No directive from God is greater than these two." The interpreter of the rules said, "Teacher, you have really answered my inquiry, because there truly is only one God. There are no others. To love him with your whole being—emotions, intellect, spiritual depth, to the limit of these capacities—and to love every other person as intensely as you love yourself supersedes every rule or ritual." When Jesus recognized his keen perception, he said, "You are on the fringe of the Spirit dimension."

MARK 12:28–34a

MOTIVE GREATER THAN PERFORMANCE

While Jesus was speaking, one of the pious rule keepers invited him to dinner. He accepted and went home with him. Because he went in directly and sat down to eat, the rule keeper was shocked, because Jesus had not performed the hand-washing ritual before the meal. Jesus said to him, "You pious rule keepers are very careful to keep your ritual cleansings, but you seldom consider your inner motivation, which is quite perverted. Fools! Did not God, who made the outside, also make the inside? But give what is in your plates and cups to the poor, and everything will be ritually clean for you."

LUKE 11:37–41

While Jesus had the ear of the rule keepers, he posed a question to them: "What are your opinions about the Messiah? Whose offspring is he?" They responded immediately, "He is the offspring of David, our king." "If that is true," Jesus asked, "why does David, by the inspiration of the Spirit of God, address the Messiah as Lord? Remember that he said in one of the psalms, 'The Lord said to my Lord, "Take your place of authority next to me until everything that contradicts you has been subdued."' Since David addressed the Messiah as his Lord, how can the Messiah be his child?" Not a rule keeper opened his mouth, and from that day on, not a one of them interrogated him again.

DAY 48

JESUS DENOUNCES THEIR PERVERSION OF THE LAW

After exposing the hypocrisy of the rule keepers, Jesus continued teaching the crowd, along with his understudies: "Those interpreters of the rules and the rule keepers themselves are successors to Moses. Listen to their instructions and do what they tell you to do, but don't imitate their actions, because they are better preachers than practitioners. For example, they pile up rules and regulations heavy as a marble slab, but they don't keep those rules any more than they lift the slab with their little finger. These pious rule keepers are professional actors. They play their parts and say their lines to elicit the desired response from their audience. You must identify them by their dress, since you could never recognize them by the way they live. That's why they like to sit at the head table during the festivals and have the front seat in the worship service. And that's why they perform ritual greetings on the street and encourage people to call them 'Teacher' or 'Instructor.' I don't want anyone to call you 'Teacher,' because there is only one teacher, the Christ. All of you are equal. You are brothers and sisters.

"Also, don't consider anyone your father on this earth in the sense that he is the source of your life, because you have only one Father who is the source of all. Don't lord it over one another. There is only one in authority over all—the Christ. Remember what I tried to teach you before: 'The greatest fulfillment of your life will come from serving one another.' The person who assumes superiority to others will evoke jealousy and anger and will be toppled, but the person who identifies with the people and participates in their life will be recognized by the Giver of life.

"Beware, you interpreters of the rules and you pious rule keepers, you actors! Beware of the fate that awaits you. You make it very difficult for persons to experience the Spirit dimension. For all your words about real life, you don't live it. Take heed to your faith, interpreters of the rules and rule keepers, you phonies! You send missionaries to the ends of the earth to convert innocent people to your way of thinking, and in so doing, you distort their lives and destroy their being.

"Beware of your fate, you blind leaders! You say, 'It's not binding if a person swears by the house of God, but if he swears by the gold in God's house, it is binding!' You are so ignorant and insensitive! Which is of more importance, the gold or the house of God that contains the gold? In the same way, you have a rule that says, 'It isn't binding if a person swears by the altar in God's house, but if anyone swears by the gift that is laid on that altar, it is binding.' You ignorant, insensitive leaders! Which has greater significance, the gift or the altar that consecrates it? Whoever swears by the altar swears by everything connected with it. Whoever swears by God's house swears not only by it but by God who dwells in it. And whoever swears by an ultimate power swears by God's authority and reality.

"Beware of your fate, you interpreters of the rules, you pious rule keepers, you phonies! Because of your interest in money, you are willing to give ten percent of tiny spices like mint and anise and cumin, but you totally reject what is really important—justice, kindness, and trust. You should give priority to these character traits without neglecting the other. You are blind leaders with inverted priorities. You choke at a gnat and swallow a camel.

"Beware of your fate, you interpreters of the rules, you pious rule keepers, you phonies! In your approach to life, you clean up the exterior, but you leave the grease and grime of extortion and impurity on the inside. You are so blind. If you clean the grease and grime that is on the inside, the external appearance will take care of itself.

"Beware of your fate, you interpreters of the law, you rule keepers, you phonies! You remind me of neatly kept, whitewashed tombstones that appear immaculate on the outside but on the inside are full of bones, death, dirt, and decay. You are careful to live according to the rules so that everything will look right to others, but surely you are aware that your performance does not spring from the heart. You live a contradiction between who you are and what you do.

"Beware of your fate, you interpreters of the rules, you rule keepers, you phonies! You are very careful to preserve the graves of the speakers for God and to identify the places where holy people have been buried. You often lament, 'If we had been contemporaries with these good and godly people, we would not have persecuted and killed the speakers for God, as our forefathers did.' In your lament, you identify yourselves as descendants of those who murdered the speakers for God. That's tantamount to a confession of what you will do. In the most complete way possible, you will carry out your forefathers' tradition of getting rid of the speakers for God. You are a group of self-deceivers, a generation of beguilers. How can you escape the consequences of the contradiction in your being? Somewhere it is written in our records, 'I will send speakers to you, persons of wisdom, interpreters of my plan. Some of these you will kill; some you will even beat in the places of worship; and others you will expel from one city after another.' And you will be held accountable for all your actions, reaching all the way back to the beginning of time when a good man, Abel, was slain, right down to Zechariah, son of Barachiah, a man who was killed in God's house right beside the altar. Honestly, the consequences for all these rejections will be visited on this generation.

MATTHEW 22:41–23:36

While he was directing his comments to the enforcers of the rules, the interpreters of the rules and the pious rule keepers attacked him, hoping he would, in the heat of argument, make statements for which they could condemn him. They kept waiting and listening intently for evidence to indict and convict him.

LUKE 11:53–54

Aware of their intent, Jesus sat down beside the collection box and observed the contributors. He noted a number of rich people making large contributions. About that time, a poverty-stricken widow came up and dropped in a couple of coins, worth about two cents. Jesus motioned to his understudies and said, "This poor widow has given more than all the wealthy contributors. They have given a token contribution from their abundance, but she out of her poverty has contributed her last cent."

MARK 12:41–44

DAY 49

A TIME OF EXTREME TESTING IS COMING

After issuing these warnings, directed toward both the pious rule keepers and his understudies, Jesus left God's house. As they left, his understudies said, "Look how big God's house is and how finely it is decorated." Jesus said, "You see how large it is and how well it is constructed. Honestly I tell you, not one stone of that building will be left in place, but the entire structure will be destroyed."

They walked out of the city, and Jesus sat down on the Mount of Olives to rest. While he was relaxing, his understudies came to him without the crowd. They said, "Tell us when God's house will be destroyed. And also, tell us about your coming again—whatever that means—and describe the climax of history."

Jesus answered, "Here are some things you need to watch for. Beware of illusions, both your own and those of other persons. While you await my return, you could be confused by delusions of those who claim to be the Christ. Many will buy their line. Before this era terminates, expect fierce wars and the threat of more. Do not be anxious for your own security but realize that wars will take place before the climax of history. There will be strife within nations, and there will be strife and war between nations. Nations will lack food; there will be plagues of insects and pests; and there will be natural calamities, such as earthquakes, in different places. These events will mark the beginning of your testing and pain.

"In addition to the general threats I have outlined, you will be arrested and tortured, and many will be killed. Sometimes you will be hated by everyone because you have associated yourself with me. During these periods of severe testing, many will turn from their relationship with me. Some will identify family members to an enemy. Others will actually hate their relatives. Many phonies will appear who claim to be God's spokespersons, and they will create a following with their delusions. Because the powers of destruction will be so intense, the motivation that love inspires will wane in many persons. But the person who perseveres to the completion of the age will find personal wholeness and fulfillment. And the good news of the Spirit dimension will be told throughout the earth, so that every nation will have an opportunity to respond to it. Only then will the climax of history come about.

A TIME TERRIBLE BEYOND WORDS

"Now, regarding the utter destruction of this house of God, whenever you see the most irreverent, unholy act imaginable—an act that Daniel, God's spokesperson, has described—transpiring in this consecrated place, if you are in Judea at that time, evacuate the city and hide in the mountains. During that crisis, take care for your own safety. Should you be on top of the house, either resting or repairing the roof, don't even come down. If you should be in the field working, don't even pick up a shirt you have pulled off. Those women who are pregnant or who are nursing babies will have a very difficult time evacuating the city with haste. Do hope and pray that the crisis does not come in winter or on the consecrated day when you cannot travel. During this time there will be great pain and suffering, misery that people have never known before and truly will never know again. This period of suffering and pain will be so intense that no human being could survive, yet for the sake of the people, God will shorten those days and preserve their lives.

HISTORY'S CLIMAX IN GOD'S HANDS

"Right after the pain and suffering of these days, you will observe strange signs in the natural order. There will be an eclipse of the sun and of the moon and a number of shooting stars, and it will appear that the sky is falling around you. At that time, God's Representative Man will appear in the heavens. Then, and only then, will all persons on earth recognize him and be sorry for their deeds. And they shall recognize the Representative Man because of his authority and power. When he arrives, he will commission his associates with the blast of the trumpet, and they will summon his people from the four corners of the earth and from the whole universe.

"Now, learn this lesson from the fig tree. When a fig tree begins to bud and send forth its leaves, you are aware that summer is not far away. Likewise, when you see all the things I have described taking place, you will know that my reappearance is very near, like someone knocking at your door. When these things take place, the people who see and experience them will not die until everything I have said has come to pass. The earth and sky may disintegrate, but the promises and predictions I have made will stand."

"But do not be led astray. No person knows exactly when the climax of history will come—I mean not a single person, not even God's special messengers, but my Father only. I instruct you, be alert every day, for you do not know the exact time when the Christ will come again.

MATTHEW 24:1–22; 29–36

"Keep a close watch over yourselves, lest your undisciplined impulses take charge and leave you groggy with drunkenness or laden with excessive commitments, and this day finds you in bondage to temporal things. The appearance of that day will be disguised like a trap, and it will catch some inhabitants of the earth off guard. Be diligent. Ask God to deliver you from all this pain and suffering and make you worthy to associate with the Representative Man."

LUKE 21:34–36

DAY 50

STAY ALERT

Again Jesus cautioned them with a story: "Reality may be compared to this story of ten bridesmaids. Five of them made proper preparation for the wedding, whereas the other five neglected to do so. Those who were foolish took their lamps full of oil, but they took none extra. Those who prepared themselves properly not only filled their lamps with oil but took extra oil. Because the bridegroom did not come immediately, all of them went to sleep. During the night there was a sudden, loud cry, 'Prepare yourselves, the bridegroom is coming! Go present yourselves to him!' All the young ladies rose, picked up their lamps, and began lighting them. Those who had not prepared themselves said to the others, 'Share your oil with us, for our lamps have gone out and we cannot light them.' To this, the others responded, 'No, we cannot share our oil with you because we will run out. Go and buy oil and come back.' Those without oil went to purchase some. While they were gone, the bridegroom came. Those who were prepared presented themselves to him, and he took them into his house. Later on, the five bridesmaids who had not prepared themselves came knocking at the door: 'Sir, sir, open the door to us also.' The bridegroom responded, 'Really, I don't know who you are,' and he would not open the door. Get the point. Stay alert at all times, because you do not know the moment when the Representative Man, like a bridegroom, will be coming for you."

MATTHEW 25:1–13

THE FINAL ACCOUNTING

Then Jesus said to his understudies, "At the climax of history you can expect the return of the Representative Man, and at that time he will take charge, and he will be accompanied by the special messengers of God. He will assemble all the nations of the earth, and he will divide them just as a shepherd separates sheep from goats. And he will place the sheep to his right and the goats to his left. Then, with God's own authority, he will beckon those on his right hand: 'Come along with me, those of you who have been fulfilled by my Father. Take your place in this ultimate form of being, a place marked out for you since the first moment of creation. You see, I was hungry and you fed me. I was thirsty and you gave me something to drink. I was unknown to you in many of our encounters and you accepted me. I was without clothes and you gave me clothes; I was sick and forsaken and you visited me. I was locked up in jail and you took time to be with me.'

"At that time, those to whom he is speaking will ask, 'Sir, when did we see you hungry and give you something to eat, or thirsty and give you something to drink? And when did we meet you as one unknown and invite you into our houses? Or when did we see you without clothes and clothe you? When did we see you sick or in jail and visit you?' And then the Representative Man, with the authority of God, will respond, 'Honestly, when you did any of those things to any human being, especially those without position or power, you were doing it to me personally.'

"With that, he will say to those on the left, 'Take your leave. Go away from me. Your being is under a curse, and you must experience the fate of all who reject the ultimate plan and purpose of God. You see, I was hungry and you didn't give me anything to eat. I was thirsty and you didn't offer me a drink. I was unknown to you and you didn't risk inviting me in. I was without clothes and you didn't give me any, sick and in jail and you never visited.' These will protest, saying, 'Sir, when did we see you hungry or thirsty or a stranger or without clothes or ill or in jail and did not respond to your need?' He will answer, 'I tell you the truth, when you had the opportunity to do these things to any human being, especially to those without position and power, and you did not do it, it was the same as not doing it to me. Those who did not relate to the needs of their fellow human beings with sensitivity and concern will suffer inestimable loss. Those who did respond will experience authentic life age after age.'"

THE PLOT AGAINST JESUS

When Jesus had spoken these words about the end of the world, he said to his understudies, "You are aware that in a couple of days we will be celebrating the feast that commemorates our nation's deliverance from Egypt, and at that time the Representative Man will be handed over to his enemies to be killed." About that time, the top religious leaders, including interpreters of the rules and the decision makers of the people, met in the executive office of the chief religious leader, whose name was Caiaphas. They struck on a plan whereby Jesus would be abducted without notice and killed. By unanimous consent they concluded, "We must not apprehend him on the feast day, because we might create a riot beyond our ability to control." It was about this time that one of Jesus' followers, Judas Iscariot, went to those same religious leaders. He said to them, "How much will you pay me to hand Jesus over to you?" They put out a contract on Jesus for about thirty silver dollars. From the time of that contract, Judas looked for a chance to hand him over to his enemies.

MATTHEW 25:31–26:5, 14–16

Each day, Jesus taught in God's house, but at night he went outside the city and slept on the Mount of Olives. And every morning, the crowd gathered early at God's house to listen to him.

LUKE 21:37–38

DAY 51

CELEBRATION IN JERUSALEM

On the day of the festival of the Passover, the day in which the sacrificial lamb was offered in celebration of the deliverance from Egypt, Jesus sent Peter and John ahead into the city, saying, "Go and prepare the festival meal for us, so that we may celebrate." They asked, "Where do you want us to prepare the meal?" He replied, "Go into the city. You will meet a man carrying a pitcher of water. Follow him into whichever house he enters and say to the owner of the house, 'Our teacher asks, "Where is the guest room where I will celebrate the deliverance from Egypt with my understudies?"'" The owner will then show you a large, furnished room on the top floor of his house. Prepare for the celebration there."

Jesus' Last Days

After the Passover meal, Jesus took a piece of bread, broke it, and said to his followers, "This is my body that is broken for you." Then he took a cup of wine from the table and said, "This is my blood that is shed for you." With these two simple acts of breaking bread and drinking wine, Jesus established the practice by which his followers until this day recall his death.

(continued)

Suggestion #10
Imagine that you are at the table with Jesus and his understudies. What do you think when he

Peter and John went and found things as Jesus had told them, so they made preparation for the celebration. At the hour appointed to celebrate the festival, Jesus sat down with his twelve chosen understudies. He began by saying, "I have had a deep, deep desire to celebrate this festival with you before I suffer and die. Actually, I will not celebrate with you like this again until the ultimate fulfillment of all things."

He then took a cup of wine, thanked God for it, and offered it to the Twelve with these words: "Share this with each other. I emphasize to you that I will not participate in the celebration again until the ultimate fulfillment of all things." He took a large piece of bread, thanked God for it, then broke it, and passed it around to all of them, saying: "This is my body, which I give for your sake. Remember me as you do this." After the meal, he picked up a cup of wine, saying, "This cup, which is poured out for you, symbolizes the new relationship between God and his people, which is ratified by the shedding of my blood."

SERVING OTHERS IS GREATNESS

Later on in the evening, they began to argue with each other about who would be most prominent. He answered them, "The royalty among the non-Jews have authority over them, and they are called 'benefactors.' But this is not the way for you to have power. Rather, let the one among you with the greatest power and authority become like a young person lacking power. Let your leaders become servants of others. Who is the greater, a guest sitting at the table or the servant who waits on the guest? It's the one sitting, of course. But I am here to be your servant. You have shared my pain and temptation with me. I assure you that I have appointed a place for you in the fulfillment, as the Father has appointed a place for me. In the

---

After the meal, he dismissed one of his followers, Judas, with the words "Whatever you are to do, do quickly." Jesus knew that Judas had made a deal with Jesus' enemies to betray him.

Then Jesus invited his followers into the garden to pray with him. He separated three of them from the others and asked them to watch and pray with him. Three times he came to check on them, and each time they were asleep. Three times Jesus

(continued)

stoops to wash your feet?

---

future, you will share fellowship with me in the Spirit dimension, and you will have authority over all twelve tribes of Israel."

LUKE 22:7–20, 24–30

After supper Jesus got up from the table, took off his clothes, and wrapped a towel around his waist. He then poured water into a pan and started washing the feet of his understudies, then drying them with the towel he had wrapped about himself. When he came to Simon Peter, Peter drew back and asked, "Lord, are you going to wash my feet?" Patiently, Jesus explained, "You don't understand what I am doing now, but later on you will." Again Peter protested, "I can't let you wash my feet." Jesus answered firmly, "If I do not wash your feet, then you are not part of my movement." "If that's the case," Peter said, "don't wash only my feet. Wash my hands and my head, too." But Jesus responded, "In the kind of bathing I'm doing, you need only to have your feet washed, and that means you are completely clean. But not all of you are clean." You see, Jesus knew which one of his understudies would betray him, and that's why he said, "Not all of you are clean."

After he had finished washing the feet of his understudies, Jesus put his clothes on and sat again at the table with them. He asked them, "Do you recognize the meaning of what I have just done to you? You address me as 'Teacher' and 'Lord,' and it's right for you to do that because that's who I am. If your Lord and teacher washes your feet, you should follow his example and wash one another's feet. Because I am a model for you, you should relate to one another as I have related to you. I tell you emphatically, an employee does not have greater prestige or power than the employer. And the one who receives instructions is never greater in authority than the one who gives them. If you understand and accept this, you will be joyously fulfilled by living that way.

---

prayed, "If it is possible, let this cup of suffering pass from me; nevertheless, not my will but yours be done." Then Judas came into the garden, kissed Jesus, and left.

In rapid succession, the Jewish leaders arrested Jesus, tried him, tortured him, and turned him over to the Romans, who executed him. The original documents give a great deal of information about the trial, the execution, and the reaction of the soldiers, Jesus' followers, the Jewish leaders, and those who were executed with him. To fully appreciate what

(continued)

A FORECAST OF BETRAYAL

"What I am about to say is not directed to all of you. I know the loyalty of most of you, but in our records there is a forecast that says, 'One of those who eats with me will turn against me.' I mention this to you in advance, so that when it happens, you may be assured that I am the one you have been expecting. Once again I tell you emphatically, the person who receives my followers whom I send, by that act receives me. And the person who receives me receives God who commissioned me." After this statement, Jesus' mood changed, and he was deeply disturbed as he said, "I tell you the truth, one of you will betray me." When his understudies heard that, they looked at one another, wondering whom he meant. One of the understudies whom Jesus especially loved was reclining next to Jesus' chest. Simon Peter nudged him, urging him to ask Jesus to identify the betrayer. So this understudy asked him, "Lord, which one of us is it?" Jesus answered, "It is the one to whom I will give this piece of bread dipped in wine." Then he dipped the bread in the pitcher of wine and handed it to Judas Iscariot, Simon's son. After Judas had eaten the bread dipped in wine, the Adversary possessed him. Jesus then instructed, "Whatever you are going to do, go ahead and get it over with." Not a single person sitting at the table understood what Jesus meant by those words. Actually, there was a bit of conjecture about it. Some thought that because Judas was the treasurer, Jesus had said, "Go, buy what we need for the festival." Others thought he was instructing him to give money to the poor. After he had eaten the bread dipped in wine, Judas got up and went out into the night.

After he had gone, Jesus turned to the remaining understudies and said, "At this moment, the Representative Man is fulfilled, and God is fulfilled

---

Jesus, the best man who ever lived, suffered unjustly, read carefully the description of what happened to him on those last days of his life on earth.

through him. If God is fulfilled through him, God will also fulfill this Representative Man in himself, and this fulfillment is imminent. I look at you as though you are children of mine, unable to take care of yourselves. I will be with you a little while longer. Later on, you will look for me, and just as I have told the Jews, 'Where I am going, right now, you can't come.' So I give you a parting word. Love each other in the same way that I have loved you. I offer you a model for your love to one another. Every person you meet will recognize that you are my understudies because you relate to one another in love."

Impulsively, Simon Peter asked, "Lord, where are you going?" Jesus answered, "I am going to a place where you cannot come right now. But later on, you will follow me there." Peter said, "Lord, why can't I come with you now? I am willing to give my life for you." Jesus answered, "Do you really think you would give up your life for me? Honestly, the rooster will not crow until you have denied three times that you even know me."

DAY 52

HOME WITH GOD

Jesus continued, "Don't be anxious about anything, even death. You have always trusted in God; now trust in me also. In my Father's presence are many places to live. If this were not the case, I would tell you. I am now going to make ready your special place in God's presence. And after I make ready for you, I will return and join you more completely to myself. I want you to be where I am, so that we may always be together. You know the place where I'm going and the directions for getting there."

Thomas exclaimed, "Lord, we don't know the place! How can we know how to get there?" Jesus said plainly, "I myself am the direction, the reality, and the true life. No one enters into the presence of my Father except through me. If you know who I am, you should have a good idea of who my Father is. And because you have related yourself to me, you not only know who my Father is, but you have actually seen him."

JESUS' RELATIONSHIP WITH THE FATHER

This stirred Philip, and he requested, "Lord, just let us glimpse the Father, and we will be satisfied." With some distress Jesus responded, "Have I spent all this time with you, Philip, and still you don't know who I am? Everyone who has seen me has already glimpsed the Father, including you. How can you say, 'Give us a glimpse of the Father'? Are you not aware that I am intimately related to the Father, and the Father has the same relationship with me? All my teachings have sprung not from me but from the Father. Trust me when I tell you that I am in complete union with the Father, and the Father is in union with me. If you won't believe me because I say it, believe me because of what I do.

"I tell you the truth, every person who really believes me and shares the relationship I have with the Father will do all that I am doing. Actually, those persons will do more than I am doing, because I am going into the immediate presence of my Father. And when I'm in his presence, every request of yours that springs out of your relationship with me, I answer. The Father will be continually fulfilled through your asking and the Son's responding. Actually, whatever you request through your relationship with me will draw my response.

PROMISE OF THE ENABLER

"Because you love me, flesh out my directives. I will then request the Father to make you aware of another presence, an Enabler who will always be with you. I'm talking about the Spirit, the essence of reality. Those who do not have a relationship with me will not know this presence, because their physical senses can't grasp it. But you are already aware of the Enabler who has been in me, and now the Enabler will reside in your depths.

"I will never forsake you, nor leave you helpless. I will come back to you. After a few hours, those who do not have a relationship with me will not see me again. But you will see me. I will pass through death and still live, and I will give you deathless life also. After my resurrection, you will be convinced that I am in union with my Father and you are in union with me and I with you. Those who understand my teachings and respond to them show their love for me. Those who love me will be the recipients of my Father's love, and I will love them and reveal my nature to them."

The other Judas (not the one who betrayed him) said, "Lord, how will you reveal yourself to us and not to those who do not have a relationship with you?" Jesus responded, "All who love me will flesh out my directives. My Father will love them, and together we will enter into their depths in an unimaginable intimacy, like making a home in them. A person who does not love me will not respond to what I have taught. I say this not on my own authority but on the authority of my Father, who has commissioned me.

"I myself have told you these things while I am still with you. Later on, the Enabler, the Holy Spirit, will be sent to you by my Father. The Enabler shares my nature and will continue my teaching, and he will quicken your memory, enabling you to recall what I have taught. On the eve of my departure, I give you my peace, a peace like no other. Don't be shaken in your confidence or be anxious about what is going to happen. Remember that I told you, 'I am going away, but I will come again to you.' If you really loved me and wanted what is best for me, you would celebrate my going to the Father, because the Father is greater in power, wisdom, and love than I. Once again, I've described these things to you before they happen, so that when they happen, you will trust what I have said. In the future, I won't be talking much with you because the Adversary who controls this evil world will make his appearance, and I have nothing to do with him. I very much want the estranged ones to know that I love the Father and that I am doing what my Father told me to do. Now, let's get going."

DAY 53

SYMBOL OF THE VINE

Hear more of Jesus' final teaching. "I am the true vine, and my Father is the vinedresser. Every offshoot from me that does not produce fruit will wither. Every offshoot that produces some fruit he will prune so that it will make more fruit. I have affirmed you, and there is a clear relationship between us. Stay in relationship with me as I will with you. Just as no offshoot from the vine can produce fruit by itself, neither can you unless you stay related to me. I am the vine. You are my offshoots. Those persons who stay closely related to me, and I to them, will be very fruitful, but severed from me, they will be barren. A person who does not stay in relationship with me will wither and will eventually be cut off. Those shoots that are cast away are gathered and stacked in a pile for burning. If you stay related to me, and if my teachings take root in you, you can pray for anything you want, and it will be given to you. My Father is fulfilled when you reproduce the life I have produced in you. This productivity will demonstrate your relationship to me. I have loved you in the same way that my Father has loved me, and you must pass on this love to others. As you flesh out my teaching, you will love others as I have loved you. I have fleshed out my Father's guidance, and I remain in his love. I've told you these things so you may have my joy, and that your joy may overflow.

"Let me emphasize my directive to you: love one another as I have loved you. Those who give up their lives for their friends show incomparable love. You are my friends when you do what I have directed. From now on, I will not refer to you as employees, because an employee doesn't know what his employer will decide. I call you my friends, because everything that my employer, my Father, has told me I have shared with you. The initiative for our relationship did not come from you but from me, and I have commissioned you to produce the same life in others that I have produced in you. I want this life to be perpetuated. So I tell you, whatever you ask the Father, he will give to you because of our relationship. Again, I emphasize that you are to love one another.

A WARNING ABOUT REJECTION

"If the persons who are not in a relationship with me reject you, know that they rejected me before they rejected you. If you lived like them, they would approve of you. But because you are different from them—because I have entered into a relationship with you—they reject you. Don't forget that I said, 'The employee is not superior to the employer.' If they have attacked me, they will attack you. If they have responded to what I have said, they will respond to what you say. They will react to you in these ways because you are related to me, and they are related neither to me nor to the one who commissioned me. If I had not revealed myself to them, they would not be guilty for their behavior, but now they have no excuse for their actions. Those who reject me and are frightened by what I represent reject my Father, too. If they had not been eyewitnesses to what I am doing, they would not be guilty. Now they have witnessed me and my Father at work and have hated both of us. They have behaved in accordance with the forecast in our record: 'Without reason they rejected me.'

"Remember, I am sending you a gift, an Enabler, the Holy Spirit, the essence of truth. The Enabler will come from the Father and will confirm who I am. When the Enabler verifies to you who I am, you will verify it to others, because you have been my companions from the beginning of my ministry.

THE WORK OF THE ENABLER

"I've told you all these things so that you will not break off our relationship when the going gets tough. Your fellow Jews will throw you out of their places of worship. Actually, they will persuade themselves that killing you is doing the will of God. They will reject you, exclude you, and kill you because they don't recognize me or my Father. I have forecast this persecution so that when it happens, you will realize that I knew it in advance. I didn't tell you about this before because I was here to support and encourage you. Now I am returning to the one who commissioned me to come to you. Not one of you so much as asked, 'Where are you going?' Yet my forecast of rejection and suffering has depressed you. I really wish you understood that my return to my Father is to your advantage. Until I do, the Enabler will not begin his enabling. As soon as I am in the presence of the Father, the Enabler will become active in you.

"When the Enabler begins his work, he will convince people of their alienation from God, of the reality of God's goodness, and of their release from guilt and punishment. Persons in the world are alienated because they have rejected a relationship with me. Nevertheless, a right relationship is available for everyone because I am going into the presence of the Father. Although you will not see me, I will continue to release persons from guilt and condemnation because the Adversary has been done away with.

"There is much more I want to talk about with you, but it is no use now, because you can't understand it. When the Enabler, the Holy Spirit, the essence of truth, enters into you, the Enabler will open all reality to you. The Holy Spirit will not present his own information but will pass on to you what has been given to him. And he will unveil the future. The Enabler will inspire reverence and worship of me, and he will place me in high esteem by revealing my true fulfillment, which the Holy Spirit will show to you when he becomes active in your life. I participate in the total reality of God, and the Spirit will communicate to you my relationship with the Father.

"Expect me to be unavailable to you for a brief period. Then you can expect me to be available to you again." The understudies, being confused, began to ask one another, "What's he talking about? What does he mean, 'a brief period, and we will not have access to him, and again in a brief period, we will'? And what does this 'going to the Father' mean?" They continued, "We just don't understand what this 'brief period' refers to." Being aware of their perplexity, Jesus asked, "Are you trying to decide what I meant when I said, 'A brief period and I will not be available to you, and then after a brief period, I will'? Let me be very clear with you. You will cry and mourn, but those who do not have a relationship with me will be glad. You will be full of sadness, but your sadness will be transformed into joy.

"Your experience will be similar to that of a woman in labor. During that time she has a great deal of pain, but as soon as her baby is born, she forgets all about the pain because of the joy of bringing a new life into the world. You're sad today, but I will see you again, and you will overflow with joy that no one can destroy. After this transpires, you won't be asking me for anything. I tell you very clearly, whatever you request the Father from our relationship, he will give it to you. Up to this time, you have not made a single request to the Father because of your relationship to me. Go ahead now and ask him, and you will receive what you want. In this relationship to him, you will experience the joy of fulfillment."

DAY 54

JESUS SPEAKS PLAINLY ABOUT THE FUTURE

Jesus elaborated, "I forecast these things with symbols, but soon I will speak clearly to you and will be explicit in my representation of the Father to you. When you personally know the Father, you will no longer make requests from him because of your relationship to me. Then I will not be asking the Father in your behalf, either. You see, my Father loves you because you have loved me and trusted that I originated in God. Though my origin was in the Father, I came into human history. Now I leave this world and return to the Father."

At that statement his understudies said, "Now you are expressing yourself clearly, and not talking in symbols. We are confident that you know everything, and none of us needs to question you any further. Because of your supreme knowledge, we are confident that you originated in God." Jesus responded, "Do you really believe that? Listen, the time will come— actually, it's here already—when I will be forsaken, and every one of you will go his own way. Even then, I will not be completely alone, because my Father is present. I have described your testing so that you may have peace through our relationship. As you relate to those who do not know me, you will have suffering, rejection, and pain. Take courage. I have experienced it and have overcome it."

JESUS PRAYS FOR HIS FOLLOWERS

After Jesus had spoken these words, he lifted his eyes heavenward and prayed, "Father, this is the time. Fulfill your Son, that your Son may fulfill you. You have given me authority over everyone so that I can give real life forever to every one of them. Authentic life age after age is knowing you, the only true God, and Jesus Christ, whom you have sent. I have fulfilled you through my life on earth, and I have completed the task for which you commissioned me. It is time, Father, for you to fulfill me with your very presence, with the kind of fulfillment I had with you before the beginning of creation.

"I've revealed your nature to the persons whom you gave me out of the inhabited world. Once they were yours, and you gave them to me. They've responded to your call. Now, at last, they have recognized that you are the source of all I have said and done. I have expressed to them the truth you have expressed to me. They have received my communication and have become confident that I originated in you and that you commissioned me. I pray for these whom you have given me. At this time, I'm not praying for all of humanity but for these few whom you have given me. They all belong to you. All the understudies belong to you, and all your people belong to me, and I am fulfilled in them. I will no longer be physically alive. They will live physically, but I am returning to you. Holy Father, maintain your relationship with those whom you have given to me, so they may be united with one another as we are. While I have been with them, I have maintained their relationship with you. I sustained every one of them except one, and that rebellious person has broken our relationship so that the record may prove accurate.

"As I return to you now, I am expressing these things to my understudies so that they may experience the joy of fulfillment. I have shared your message with them, and all those people who are not related to me have rejected them because they don't fit into their culture, even as I don't. Don't take them out of the world, but keep them safe from the Adversary's power. They don't fit in any more than I do. Keep them related to you through your presence. Your message is reality. Just as you have commissioned me to enter into history, I commissioned them to carry on my work. Because of my love for them, I clarify and unify my relationship with you, that they also may be deeply aware of and related to your presence.

"I pray not only for these understudies of mine who are with me but for all who will eventually trust me because of their message to them. I pray that all of those who believe in me will be perfectly united, just as you, Father, are in an intimate relationship with me and I am in the same relationship with you. I ask that all of them will always be in an intimate relationship with us, so that eventually all people will believe that you commissioned me. The fulfillment I have in relation to you, these persons have in relation to me. I want them to be united, just as we are. This unity will be achieved by my being in them and your being in me, that they may be completely united. This unity will enable all persons to be confident that you have sent me and that you have loved all of them as you have loved me. Also, Father, I want those who have entered into a relationship with me to be with me. May they see for themselves the fulfillment that you have shared with me because you loved me before the dawn of creation. O Father, who makes all things right, humankind has not known you, but I have always known you, and my followers have become aware that you commissioned me. I have expressed to them your very nature, and I will continue to express it so that the kind of love you have given me will fulfill them, and I will live in them."

JOHN 13:4–17:26

He then queried his understudies, "When I sent you on that trip without a purse, without a money bag, and without shoes, did you suffer because you lacked necessities?" They replied, "We certainly did not." "Well, I'm changing my instructions to you now. If you have a purse, take it with you. If you have a money bag, take it. If you don't have a means of protecting yourself, sell your clothes to buy a sword. I am warning you that the forecast in our records will come to pass in me, 'And he was counted one of the sinners.' You see, everything pertaining to me will come to an end." Out of their anxiety, the understudies responded, "Lord, we have two swords." And he said, "That's enough."

DAY 55

JESUS AGONIZES THROUGH THE NIGHT

As Jesus ended this teaching, he went to the Mount of Olives, along with his understudies. Arriving there, he said to them, "Pray that you will not be tested." He went away from them about a stone's throw, fell down on his knees, and began praying, "Father, if there is any way, spare me from the horror I am facing; however, more than I want to be spared, I want your purpose to be fulfilled."

Then a heavenly messenger from God appeared, offering strength to Jesus. He was in agony and prayed with such intensity that his sweat appeared to be blood dripping on the ground. When he finished his prayer, he returned to the understudies, only to find them sleeping off their grief. He said to them, "Why are you sleeping? You should be praying that you will not be tested."

BETRAYED IN JERUSALEM

Even as he was talking, a crowd of people led by Judas, one of the understudies, approached. Judas came up as if to kiss Jesus, but Jesus said, "Judas, are you going to betray God's Representative Man with a kiss?" When his understudies caught on to what was taking place, they asked, "Lord, shall we take our swords to these people?" One of the understudies did grab his sword and strike an employee of a religious official, cutting off his right ear. But Jesus reprimanded him, saying, "Enough of that behavior!" He touched the man's ear, and it was healed. Then he spoke to the religious leaders, the officers of the Jewish house of worship, and the national rulers, all of whom had come with the crowd to apprehend him: "With these swords and clubs, it appears that you have come for a hardened criminal. Yet I taught daily in God's house, and you made no attempt to seize me. This is your big moment—the time when the forces of evil take over."

LUKE 22:35–53

PETER'S EMPHATIC DENIALS

With that, the leader of the group whom the Jews had sent arrested Jesus and tied him up. They first took him to Annas. (The chief religious official, Caiaphas, had married his daughter.) Caiaphas was the one who told the Jews that it was proper for one person to die for other people.

When they arrested Jesus, Simon Peter and another understudy followed them. The unnamed understudy was an acquaintance of the chief religious official, so he entered the leader's house with Jesus. Peter was left standing at the door. The other understudy, however, spoke to the girl who guarded the door, and she permitted Peter to come in. This same girl, being observant, said to Peter, "Aren't you one of this man's understudies?" "No," he answered quickly, "I certainly am not." Inside were some employees and officials who had built a fire because it was cold. As they stood around the fire warming themselves, Peter edged into the group and warmed himself.

The chief religious official began questioning Jesus about his understudies and his teaching. Jesus asserted, "I taught everyone without hiding what I had to say. I even taught in your places of worship and in God's house, where all the Jews go. I have said nothing secretly that I have not said openly. So why are you asking me? Why not ask those who have heard me, because they know what I have been saying?" When Jesus did not answer the religious official directly, one of the officers standing next to him slapped him, asking, "Do you respond to our official like that?" Jesus answered, "If I have been wrong in defense, tell me where. But if I have answered properly, why did you slap me?" With that, Annas ordered the soldiers to keep him bound and to take him to Caiaphas, the chief religious official.

JOHN 18:12–24

JESUS AND CAIAPHAS

Caiaphas was waiting with the interpreters of the rules and the civil officials. Peter had followed along at the edge of the crowd until they got to the home of Caiaphas. Then he stood in the yard with some of the soldiers to see what would happen. All the religious leaders who were gathered inside tried to find persons to testify against Jesus, that is, to lie under oath so convincingly that he could be given the death sentence. Though they found persons willing to testify, their stories contradicted each other. Finally, two of the witnesses agreed. They said, "We heard this man Jesus say that he could destroy God's house, then rebuild it in three days." On hearing this, Caiaphas turned to Jesus and asked, "What do you have to say about that? Can you defend your statement?" But Jesus didn't say a word. Caiaphas prodded him, saying, "In God's name, I order you to tell me if you are the Messiah, the Son of God." This time Jesus answered, "You have said so. But I tell you, in the future you will see the Representative Man expressing the authority of God and radiating the energy of the Spirit dimension."

Then Caiaphas tore his clothes in anger and shouted, "Blasphemy! We don't need to hear from anyone else. You have heard his sacrilegious boast. What shall we do to him?" Others at the court answered, "Kill him! Kill him!" Then they started spitting on Jesus, beating him and slapping him. Taunting, they asked, "If you have the powers of God's Son, tell us who hit you!"

MATTHEW 26:57b–68

Meanwhile, as Peter stood around the fire, getting warm, they asked him, "Are you one of this man's understudies?" "No," he replied emphatically, "I surely am not." Another employee of the chief religious official, who was kin to the man whose ear Peter cut off, said, "Didn't I see you with him in the garden?" Again Peter denied it, and at that moment he heard a rooster crow.

JOHN 18:25–27

DAY 56

QUESTIONED FURTHER

As the next day began to dawn, the national leaders, the prominent religious officials, and the interpreters of the rules held a conference with Jesus. They asked him, "Are you the Messiah?" He responded, "If I answer your question, you won't accept what I say. Furthermore, if I ask you pointed questions, you will not respond to them. No matter what I say, you will not release me. After this ordeal, the Representative Man will be exalted into the presence of God to share his power."

In unison, they asked him, "Are you the Son of God?" He responded, "That's who you say I am." With that they attacked him, saying, "We don't need any further evidence because we have heard his confession with our own ears."

TRIAL IN JERUSALEM

After trying to force a confession from Jesus, the council that had gathered to accuse him took him to Pilate and began laying out their evidence: "This man is a threat to our nation. He is gathering followers and instructing them not to pay taxes to Rome, and he is claiming to be our Messiah, a ruler."

LUKE 22:66–23:2

Pilate then went into the courtroom and demanded of Jesus, "Are you the ruler of the Jews?" Jesus countered, "Is this a question you thought of by yourself, or did it come from someone else?" Avoiding his question, Pilate said, "I am no Jew. The chief leaders from your own nation handed you over to me. Just what have you done?" Seeming to answer his former question, Jesus said, "My authority and dominion are not of a secular nature. If they were, my friends and associates would fight for me to deliver me from the Jews. But at this time, my dominion is not of this kind." Pilate persisted, "Are you then a king?" Jesus declared, "You keep saying that I am a king. I was born and came into this world in order to communicate reality. Everyone who participates in reality recognizes the truth of what I am saying." Pilate asked plaintively, "What is reality?"

JOHN 18:33–38a

After examining him, Pilate said to the prominent religious leaders and to the crowd that had assembled, "I see nothing criminal about this man." They persisted in their accusation: "He is going throughout our nation creating unrest, inflaming the people from Galilee to Jerusalem." When they mentioned Galilee, Pilate inquired if Jesus was a Galilean. When he learned that Jesus came from Galilee, he realized that the case belonged to Herod's jurisdiction. He ordered them to take Jesus to Herod, who at the time was in Jerusalem.

Herod was really eager to see Jesus; he had wanted to meet him for a long time. He had heard about the miraculous deeds Jesus had been performing and wanted to see him do a miracle. He began questioning Jesus, but Jesus didn't say a word to him. The prominent religious officials and the interpreters of the rules made their case against him. Then Herod and his soldiers discounted Jesus, ridiculed him, and mockingly dressed him in an expensive robe and sent him back to Pilate. And that day, Pilate and Herod once again became friends, even though they had been hostile to each other for a long time.

CONDEMNED IN JERUSALEM

After Jesus was brought back to him, Pilate summoned the prominent religious officials and the national rulers and the people. He said to them, "You have accused this man of stirring up the people. I have examined him and found him innocent of your accusations. Nor did Herod find anything for which he deserves the death penalty. I will punish him and release him."

LUKE 23:4–16

It was customary at the Jewish celebration of deliverance from Egypt for Pilate to release one prisoner chosen by the people. At the time, they held in custody a notorious criminal named Jesus Barabbas. While Pilate was talking to Jesus and the religious leaders, a huge crowd gathered to witness the prisoner's release. Pilate then asked, "Whom do you desire that I set free today? Jesus Barabbas or Jesus who calls himself the Christ?" Pilate had recognized the eagerness of the Jewish leaders to get rid of Jesus because they were envious of his influence and popularity. Pilate went over and sat down on the bench at which he made official pronouncements. While he was sitting there, he received a note from his wife that read, "Don't make any decisions about that innocent man. Because of him, my dreams have been disturbed of late." While Pilate was reading the note, the religious leaders convinced the crowd that they should request the release of Jesus Barabbas and demand the crucifixion of Jesus. After he read his wife's note, the governor turned to the crowd and asked, "Which of these two men do you want me to release today?" Instantly they said, "Barabbas." Then Pilate asked, "What do you wish me to do with Jesus who calls himself the Christ?" With a roar they shouted, "Kill him!" "Why," Pilate asked, "what has he done wrong?" Ignoring his question, they began to chant, "Kill him, kill him, kill him!"

When Pilate realized that he could not change their minds, he took a pan of water and washed his hands in the presence of the chanting crowd. Symbolically he was declaring, "I am washing my hands of all responsibility in the death of this innocent person, and I want you to know that." The people declared, "Let the responsibility for his death be on us and on our children." Pilate handed Jesus Barabbas over to them, and when he had ordered Jesus to be beaten, he then ordered his crucifixion.

MATTHEW 27:15–26

THE BETRAYER HAS A CHANGE OF HEART

By this time Judas, who had turned Jesus over to the Jewish authorities, was feeling guilty and condemning himself. He changed his mind about his deal and took the thirty silver dollars back to the leaders. "I am wrong because I have handed over to you a man who is innocent," he pleaded. But they rejected him coldly, saying, "Your guilt is of no concern to us. It's your problem!" With his heart full of regret, Judas threw down the thirty silver dollars on the temple floor, walked out, and committed suicide.

When the religious leaders had gathered up the money, they said, "It's not proper for us to place this money back in our treasury, because it has been payoff money resulting in the death of a man." After consulting a while, they decided to buy a plot of ground on the edge of the city in which to bury strangers. And from that day until this, that plot of ground has been called the Field of Blood, because of the money that was paid for an innocent man's death. There was a prediction of all this from one of God's spokesmen, Jeremiah, when he said, "And they took the thirty silver dollars, the price that was paid for his betrayal, the value that the nation of Israel had placed on him, and they bought a burial plot for strangers, as the Lord had intended."

MATTHEW 27:3–10

On Pilate's orders, the soldiers led Jesus into the assembly hall and gathered the whole battalion around him. They stripped off his clothes and dressed him in a scarlet robe. Then they plaited a crown made of thorns and pressed it on Jesus' head. In his right hand they placed a reed, like a scepter, and they began bowing to him like a king and mocking him, say-

---

The Risen Lord

Both the Jewish leaders and the Romans considered the execution of Jesus to be the end of the matter. But after Jesus had been two nights in the grave, an amazing thing happened. Jesus arose from the dead! His followers actually saw him! They talked with him, ate with him, and received instructions about what they were to do.

(continued)

Suggestion #11
Imagine yourself at the cross looking at his suffering and listening to his words from the cross. Spend some time

ing, "Hail to the chief, the king of the Jews!" They continued to taunt Jesus and spit in his face. Taking the reed out of his hand, they beat him over the head with it.

When the soldiers had finished their mockery, they took away the scarlet robe, put his own clothes back on him, and began a long procession out to the place where he was to be killed. On the way, they pulled a man out of the crowd, Simon of Cyrene, and they made him carry Jesus' cross.

MATTHEW 27:27–32

DAY 57

JESUS IS CRUCIFIED

They took charge of Jesus and led him away. Carrying his cross on his back, he went out to Golgotha, which means "the Place of the Skull." There they placed him on a cross and raised it between two other men, who were also crucified.

Pilate printed a sign and nailed it on Jesus' cross. The sign read "Jesus of Nazareth, the King of the Jews." A number of Jews read the sign. Since Jesus was crucified in a cosmopolitan city, the sign was printed in three languages: Hebrew, Greek, and Latin. The top religious leaders went to Pilate, saying, "Don't write 'the King of the Jews.' Rather say, 'This man said, I am the king of the Jews.'" But Pilate refused, saying, "Let the sign stand the way I have written it."

After the soldiers placed Jesus on the cross, they divided his clothes into four stacks, one for each soldier. This also included his robe, which didn't have a seam in it but rather was woven throughout from top to bottom. As the soldiers discussed what to do with his robe, they agreed, "Let's not cut

---

The encounters the band of followers had with Jesus after his death were numerous. Mary, a woman Jesus had liberated, went to his tomb on the first day of the week to take spices, much as we take flowers to express our respect and love for someone who has died. While she was crying, Jesus spoke to her. At first she thought him to be the gardener, but when he said her name, Mary recognized Jesus.

He sent her to tell his followers that he was alive with this meditation.

(continued)

---

it; instead, let's shoot dice to see whose it will be." They did as had been forecast in the record, "They divided my clothes among them, and they gambled for my robe." So they rolled the dice and divided his possessions.

Meanwhile, standing near Jesus' cross were his mother; his aunt, Mary the wife of Clopas; and Mary Magdalene. When Jesus recognized his mother and that special understudy whom he loved standing beside her, he said, "Mother, this is your son." Then he said to the understudy, "This is your mother." From that time on, that understudy took her into his own home.

JOHN 19:16–27

Along with Jesus, two criminals were killed. At the Place of the Skull, they nailed Jesus to the cross and placed one criminal on his right and one on the left. Jesus prayed, "Father, do not hold these acts against them, because they are not aware of what they are doing." The crowd stood around the cross watching him suffer. Then the national rulers began mocking him again: "He delivered others, let him deliver himself, if he is the Messiah chosen by God." The soldiers also joined in the mockery, offering him sour wine and saying, "If you are the ruler of the Jews, deliver yourself."

One of the criminals hanging beside Jesus said, "If you are the Messiah, deliver yourself and us." The other criminal said, "Don't you have any respect for God, even while you are dying like this man? We deserve to be punished for what we have done, but he has done nothing wrong." Then speaking to Jesus he said, "Lord, please consider me when you come into power." Jesus answered him, "Listen, this very day you will be with me in God's presence."

LUKE 23:32–43

---

and where to meet him. She went in haste, hardly believing what her eyes had seen.

One striking story about his risen and living presence comes from the report of two of his followers who were returning to the village of Emmaus from Jerusalem. As they were walking along, deep in thought about the execution of Jesus and the strong reports that he was alive, Jesus himself joined them on their journey, but they did not recognize him.

Jesus asked them about themselves. Somewhat insulted, they retorted, "Are you the only one who does not know what has happened

(continued)

About noon, the sun was eclipsed, and it was dark until about three in the afternoon. At the hour of prayer, Jesus cried aloud, "My God, my God, why have you left me alone?" His words were misunderstood by those who stood nearby; they thought he was calling for Elijah.

MATTHEW 27:45–47

About this time, Jesus cried out at the top of his voice, "Father, I surrender my spirit to you!" Later, when Jesus knew his mission finished, he said, "I am thirsty." This was to comply with the forecast in the record.

Those who were killing him had a container full of vinegar. They dipped a sponge, placed it on a stick, and pressed it on his lips. After they had given him the vinegar, Jesus said, "It is finished." His head dropped, and he died.

LUKE 23:46a; JOHN 19:28–30

At the death of Jesus, the veil in the temple that separated the masses from the immediate presence of God ripped apart. Jesus' death was also accompanied by an earthquake and a disruption of the forces of nature. The earthquake opened the graves of many holy persons who died long ago. After Jesus' resurrection, these came out of the graves and went into Jerusalem and showed themselves. When the Roman soldier and the others who were standing around looking at Jesus felt the earthquake and heard the shouting, they were frightened and said, "In reality, this must have been the Son of God."

MATTHEW 27:51–54

Because it was the day of preparation for their rest day, the Jews did not want bodies left on the crosses. They requested that Pilate break the legs of the victims and take their bodies down. Thus, the soldiers came and broke the legs of the two who had been crucified with Jesus. But they did not break his legs, because he was already dead. One of the soldiers, how-

---

in Jerusalem these last three days?" (In fact, he was the only one who did.) Jesus spoke of the fact that Christ had to suffer and rise from the dead, but they were not ready to hear his words.

When they arrived at the village, Jesus seemed to be going on, but they insisted that he come in. After the long walk, they sat down to eat. Jesus took the bread, gave thanks, and broke it. And as he broke the bread, their eyes were opened and they recognized him. Then he vanished.

Quickly, they made the long trip back to Jerusalem to tell the other followers how their hearts burned within them as Jesus talked to them

(continued)

ever, stabbed Jesus' side with a spear, and immediately blood and water gushed out. (The one writing saw what happened and testifies to it, and he is telling the truth so that you may believe.) They omitted breaking Jesus' legs so that the forecast in the record would be accurate: "Not a bone in his body will be broken." And there is another statement in the record that says, "They will look at him whom they have pierced."

For fear of the Jews, Joseph from Arimathea was a secret understudy of Jesus. After all these things had happened, he asked Pilate for permission to remove the body of Jesus from the cross. Receiving permission, Joseph came and took the body of Jesus. He was accompanied by Nicodemus, the man who came to Jesus during the night for advice. Nicodemus brought along a mixture of spices, actually about one hundred pounds. These two removed the body of Jesus and wrapped it in a linen cloth, then covered it with spices the way the Jews customarily bury their dead. Near the place where Jesus was killed was a garden, and in the garden was a new tomb that had never been used. Because this was the day before the festival, they placed Jesus' body in the cavelike tomb.

JOHN 19:31–42

The day after killing Jesus, the religious leaders, along with the pious rule keepers, asked for a conference with Pilate. They stated, "We remember what this impostor said when he was alive. He declared, 'After three days, I will experience resurrection.' Please issue an order that guards be placed at the cave where he is buried until after the third day. This will prevent his followers from stealing the body during the night and declaring to the people, 'He has risen from the dead.' This latter error would certainly be worse than the former." Pilate agreed and said, "Since you have sentries who can guard the cave, you have my permission to guard it as carefully as

---

on the road and how he was made known to them as he broke the bread. And this story has inspired every follower of Jesus to expect his presence on the road and to look for him in the broken bread and poured wine.

Later that same day, the two men who had seen Jesus on the road went to their companions in Jerusalem. After they had told their story to this group of followers, Jesus came to them while they were eating. Without announcement, he appeared in their midst. He spoke, ate, and drank with them to assure them that he was not a ghost.

(continued)

you can." So these Jewish leaders went out to the tomb, sealed the entrance, and placed guards there.

MATTHEW 27:62–66

DAY 58

RESURRECTION TO ASCENSION

Before daybreak on the first day of the week, Mary Magdalene came to the grave and found that the stone that had sealed the entrance had been removed. She dashed off and met Simon Peter and the understudy who was especially loved by Jesus. She exclaimed, "They have removed the Lord from the cave, and I don't know what they have done with him!" Peter and his companion rushed to the cave. For a while they ran along together, and then the beloved understudy outran Peter to the cave. Bending down to look inside, he saw the linen cloth in which the body of Jesus had been wrapped. However, he didn't go in. About that time, Simon Peter got to the cave and saw the linen cloth also. He noted that the napkin which had been tied around Jesus' head was not stacked with the linen cloth but neatly folded and laid to one side. Peter's companion then came into the cave and, looking around, had faith that Jesus was alive. At this point, Jesus' teaching about resurrection had not fully dawned on them. After this, Peter and his companion went back home.

Mary remained at the cave and stood outside crying. In the midst of her grief, she bent over and peered into the cave. Sitting at each end of the slab on which Jesus' body had lain were messengers of God, clothed in white. They asked, "Woman, why are you crying?" Mary replied, "Because someone has removed my Lord's body, and I don't know where they have put it."

One of the men who followed Jesus was named Thomas. When he heard the testimony of the others about Jesus being alive, he could not believe it. Thomas said, "Unless I see the nail prints in his hands and thrust my hand into his side where the spear pierced him, I will not believe." Thomas, like many who were to follow, needed verification—seeing, feeling, hearing for himself.

Again, Jesus appeared to the little band of followers, and this time Thomas was with them. Jesus said to Thomas, "Put your finger in the nail prints; thrust your hand in my side. See that it is I."

(continued)

With that, she turned around and saw Jesus standing behind her, but she did not recognize him. He asked, "Woman, why are you crying? For whom are you looking?" Thinking him the gardener, she replied, "Sir, if you have removed his body, tell me where you put it, and I will take care of it." Then Jesus gently uttered her name, "Mary." She turned around and cried out joyfully, "Teacher!" Jesus instructed her, "Don't cling to me, because I have not yet gone into the presence of my Father, but I want you to deliver a message to my brothers. Say to them, 'I return into the immediate presence of my Father and your Father, my God and your God.'" As he instructed her, Mary Magdalene reported to the understudies that she had seen the Lord, and she gave them his message.

JOHN 20:1–18

While the women were reporting to the understudies, the guards who had been at the cave went to the city and told the religious leaders everything that had happened. When the leaders consulted with the guards, they gave them a large payment of hush money and instructed them to say, "His followers came during the night while we were asleep and stole his body." The leaders also told the guards, "If for any reason this report comes back to the governor, we will intervene on your behalf and make sure that nothing happens to you." The guards took the money and told the story as they were instructed. And this is how the Jews continued to explain the disappearance of Jesus' body.

MATTHEW 28:11–15

HOPE FOR UNDERSTUDIES

On that very day, two of Jesus' followers were walking toward Emmaus, which is about seven miles from Jerusalem. On the way, they were dis-

---

Thomas said, "My Lord and my God!"

Jesus spoke enduring words to Thomas: "Because you have seen, you have believed. How blessed are those who have not seen and yet believe."

---

cussing the events of the last few days. While they were talking to each other and raising questions about those events, Jesus joined them on their journey. Although they saw him physically, they didn't recognize who he was. Eventually, he asked them, "What are you fellows talking about as you walk along?" They just stood there, looking sad. Cleopas, one of the two, finally replied, "Are you the only visitor to Jerusalem who is unaware of the things that have happened these last few days?" And Jesus asked, "What things are you referring to?"

"We are referring to Jesus of Nazareth, who showed by his words and deeds that he was a messenger of God. And we were discussing how our prominent religious officials and national rulers accused and indicted him and had him killed. We believed he would liberate our nation. We were also discussing the fact that this is the third day since he was killed, and we were expecting something special today. We are confused by a report from the women in our fellowship who said the grave was empty. Earlier this morning they went to the grave but didn't find the body. They reported to us that they had seen special messengers from God who assured them that he is alive. And we were further confounded because a group of our companions went out to the grave and discovered the women had reported accurately. But they didn't see him alive."

Jesus said to them, "You have such a distorted picture of reality, and you are slow to believe what God's spokespersons have said. Don't you understand that the Christ was meant to experience all these things and then enter into his ultimate fulfillment?" Then Jesus began with the Jewish law and proceeded through the writings of God's spokespersons as he explained to them everything that had been written in the record about himself.

Jesus: Present in the Spirit

On the eve of his departure from the earth, Jesus instructed his followers to wait in Jerusalem to receive his promise of presence. About 120 waited in prayer. After ten days, the whole group experienced something like a whirling wind, then a burning like fire, and then a fullness created by their consciousness of the divine presence. The metaphors of wind

(continued)

Suggestion #12
Read the story of Thomas on pages 159–60. Close your eyes and imagine that you have that same conversation with

By this time, they were getting close to their destination, and Jesus continued on his way. When they noted that he was going on, they called to him and invited him in. "Stay here with us, because this day is nearly over." He accepted their invitation and entered their house. While they were eating supper, he picked up a piece of bread, thanked God for it, broke it, and shared it with each of them. As he broke the bread, their eyes were opened and they recognized him; and in that instant, he disappeared. Then they confessed to each other that their hearts had burned within them while he talked with them on the road, explaining the meaning of the ancient writings. Without going to bed, they headed straight back to Jerusalem to find the eleven understudies and their friends. When they arrived, the Eleven said, "Truly the Lord has experienced resurrection and has revealed himself to Simon." Then they described their experience on the way to Emmaus and how they recognized him when he broke the bread.

DAY 59

BEYOND JERUSALEM

As they were reporting on the breaking of bread, Jesus revealed himself in their midst. The group was frightened out of their wits, thinking they were seeing a ghost. Then Jesus asked, "Why are you distressed, and why are you thinking these things? Look at my hands. Look at my feet. Be convinced that it is truly I. Touch me and see for yourself, because a ghost does not have flesh and bones as you see me having." After this bold declaration, he showed them his hands and his feet. Because they were so overwhelmed with joy, they couldn't believe what they were seeing. While they were absorbed in joy and wonderment, he asked, "Have you any food?" They

and fire are efforts to reduce to language the powerful experience of encountering the presence of the risen Jesus Christ.

These followers praised God as they experienced these ecstatic manifestations of the other dimension, the Holy. As they reflected on this experience, they realized that it was like Jesus being with them when they gathered together, even residing in the consciousness of each. The one who had been with

(continued)

Jesus. Listen for the words that come to you.

shared with him a piece of broiled fish and witnessed him eating it. Then Jesus said, "I told you all about these things when I was training you. I described how everything about me in the rules that Moses gave and the explanations the spokespersons made of me and even the references to me in our prayer book had to come to pass." He continued talking to them and quickening their understanding so that they could grasp the meaning of sacred texts. He explained to them, "It is clearly taught in the records that the Messiah must experience pain and rejection, be killed, and experience resurrection on the third day. It is also taught that all people, beginning here in Jerusalem, should be told that they have an opportunity to change their attitudes and behavior, getting a new start in life, with their past blotted out. You have seen these things come to pass. It is my intention to send you a gift from my Father. Wait here in Jerusalem until you receive that spiritual Enabler from God."

LUKE 24:13–49

His understudies were jubilant when they recognized that he was the Lord. Jesus repeated his greeting, "Peace is yours." Then he said, "Just as my Father has commissioned me, I am commissioning you." Then he breathed on them, speaking these words: "Receive the Holy Spirit. Every person's sins you forgive will be completely forgiven. Those whom you do not forgive will remain unforgiven."

THOMAS DEMANDS PROOF

At the first appearance of Jesus to his understudies after resurrection, Thomas, the twin, was absent and consequently did not see Jesus. Later on, those who did said to Thomas, "We saw the Lord and he is alive." Thomas declared, "I don't believe it. And I won't believe it until I see the

---

them in the flesh, teaching and guiding them, was now in them; the Spirit of Jesus Christ had taken up residence in their deep consciousness, even as he had promised.

These men and women who were filled with the awareness of Christ's presence began to tell the story of his life and ministry. They repeated his sayings. They talked about their experiences of seeing and hearing him after he was executed and came back to life.

The telling of the simple stories had an amazing power. Merely telling the story penetrated the consciousness of the hearers so that they

(continued)

---

nail holes in his hands and put my finger into them. Until I place my hand into his side, I won't believe it." A week later, the understudies assembled and again locked all the doors for security, but this time Thomas was there. With the doors locked, Jesus suddenly stood in their midst and said, "Peace is yours." He spoke directly to Thomas, "Put your finger into my hands, and place your hand in my side. Don't doubt. Believe!" Thomas replied spontaneously, "You are my Lord! You are my God!" "You believe because you have personally seen me, Thomas," Jesus stated, "but how fulfilled will those be who have not seen me personally yet still believe."

And Jesus offered additional proof of who he was to his understudies. He did many things, most of which are not in this story. The incidents that are recorded here are written so that you may believe that Jesus is the Messiah, the Son of God, and in believing, you will have life through him.

DAY 60

"NURTURE MY FOLLOWERS"

Later on, Jesus came again to his understudies. This time they were by the Sea of Tiberias. Those gathered included Simon Peter, Thomas the twin, Nathanael from Cana in Galilee, the sons of Zebedee, and a couple of other understudies. Simon had said to these men, "I'm going fishing." "We want to go, too," they said. They left immediately, got into a ship, and fished all night, but they didn't catch anything.

In the early daylight hours, they saw someone standing on the shore but did not realize it was Jesus. Then Jesus called to them, "Have you caught anything?" "No, we haven't," they answered back. He suggested, "Throw

---

themselves felt a connection with Christ. Verbalizing the story with their conviction seemed to bridge the gap between the seen and unseen worlds, between the time Jesus was personally present in the flesh and the time he is present in the Spirit.

When persons who had not been followers of Christ heard the story, it opened them to the Spirit dimension of existence. In that state of openness, they encountered the risen Jesus Christ, and through this encounter they entered into a personal relationship with Christ. This relationship with Christ made them equal participants in the gatherings

(continued)

your net on the right side of the boat and see what you catch." They threw the net as he had instructed, and it got so full of fish they couldn't draw it in. Then the understudy whom Jesus especially loved said to Peter, "That's the Lord." When Simon Peter realized that it was indeed the Lord, he slipped into his clothes, because he had been nearly naked. Then he jumped overboard and started making his way to land. The other disciples followed in the boat, dragging the net full of fish. They were about a hundred yards from shore.

As soon as they landed, they saw a nice bed of coals with fish and bread already on it. Then Jesus requested, "Bring me some of your fish." Simon Peter went over and pulled in the net filled with large fish. Although the catch was exactly 153 fish, the net was not broken. He took some of the fish to Jesus. Then Jesus invited them, "Come on, let's eat." Not a single understudy asked, "Who are you?" because they knew he was the Lord. Jesus served them with bread and fish. This experience was the third time Jesus revealed himself to the understudies after he had experienced resurrection.

While they were eating, Jesus asked Simon Peter, "Simon, son of John, do you love me completely?" He responded, "Yes, Lord, you know that I love you." Jesus said to him, "Then nurture my followers." He asked him a second time, "Simon, son of John, do you love me completely?" Again he said, "Yes, Lord, you know that I love you." Again Jesus said, "Nurture my followers." A third time he asked, "Simon, son of John, are you certain you love me?" Peter was distressed because of the way Jesus phrased his question the third time, "Do you love me?" Peter answered, "Lord, you know everything about me. You know that I love you." Then Jesus said again, "Nurture my followers. I tell you very clearly, Peter, when you were a young

of those who were Christ's original followers. Through the teaching of the first followers, through fellowship with the others, and through prayer, the next generation came to know Jesus more fully. He lived in this new community of persons just as he had lived in his own flesh.

This Jesus story concludes with his telling his followers to give witness to him—his teaching, healing, dying, and rising—and as they obey his *(continued)*

Suggestion #13

Read in a meditative way the account of Jesus' final conversation with his followers (Luke 24:36ff.; Acts 1:3–11;

man, you dressed yourself and went wherever you wanted to. But when you get to be old, you will stretch out your hands, and another will take you to a place you don't want to go." Jesus was describing Peter's death, which would fulfill God's purpose. After he had instructed him, he said to Peter, "Follow me."

JOHN 20b–21:19

All eleven remaining understudies followed Jesus to a mountain nearby. There they worshiped him, though some still doubted. Jesus came close and spoke to them: "Complete authority has been given to me throughout the universe. I commission you to go into every nation on earth and teach everyone what I have taught you. Join them to your community of faith by baptizing them in the name of the Father, the Son, and the Holy Spirit. Teach them to obey all my instructions, and be assured I will be with you always in everything, until the climax of history."

MATTHEW 28:16–20

And while he was in the middle of blessing them, he disappeared from their sight and went into the immediate presence of God. They returned to Jerusalem ecstatic with joy and were continually in God's house, praising and worshiping him.

LUKE 24:51–53

directive, he promises to be with them, even in them. Today we stand on the frontier with the commission to keep telling the story of the greatest man who ever lived, Jesus, the Son of God.

Will you become one of the witnesses?

see pages 156–59), and see if he calls you to share in the task of witness to the world.

QUESTIONS PEOPLE ASK

As we meet with people in our regular work, they ask questions about Jesus Christ and how we know him today. We have selected some of the common questions that are asked and have answered them from the perspective of the Jesus story.

I

Q. What is the difference between having a personal relationship with Jesus Christ and having one with Michelangelo or St. Paul?

A. Both Michelangelo and St. Paul were great persons in their day, but both of them are dead. Jesus Christ is alive and present to us today!

II

Q. Isn't it presumptuous to speak of having a personal relationship with God?

A. Yes, unless you believe the gospel (the good news). If this relationship were our own creation or merit, it would be the height of presumption to think that we earn the right to be personally related to God. But if we believe the good news Jesus Christ taught about God, that God desires a personal relationship with each of us, as intimate as a good father-child relationship, it is not presumptuous to claim a personal relationship with God.

III

Q. What am I to do when there is an emptiness inside and a longing for something—but I don't know what?

A. Ultimately, the longing inside is a longing for God.

A long time ago, Augustine said, "O God, you have made us for yourself and our hearts are restless until they rest in you."

All of us have deep longings. We long for security, a feeling of belonging, self-worth, and the achievement of something worthwhile in our lives. All these longings can be fulfilled temporarily on a purely human plane, but ultimately this fulfillment fails us because it is bound by time.

Probably the best way to begin this search for fulfillment will be to pray or continue your prayer. Prayer opens you to God and to the source of fulfillment for your deepest hungers.

IV

Q. Is our search for God something we choose, or is it part of God's plan?

A. Both!

The search is for something beyond ourselves, the missing link in life, the unfulfilled dream of what we were meant to be. In short, it is a search for God.

From the Jewish-Christian perspective, the search is for "something" that was lost. Human life was created in the image of God; Eden was a symbol of unity, peace, and perfect fulfillment. But we humans turned toward material things for our fulfillment rather than toward God, and we, like Adam, were expelled from the garden.

Ever since we left Eden, we've been trying to go back. Strange thing is, we can never go back! The novelist Thomas Wolfe was right: "You can't go home again." At least, you can't go back to Eden. Home is in the future; home is the hope we have for being with God in the new heaven and the new earth.

Your destiny lies before you. Go for it!

V

Q. Can this longing or hunger for God be fulfilled while one maintains a "normal" life, or does it require quitting your job and going to a monastery?

A. God does not make us weirdos. Life with God is for common, ordinary people who work every day, marry, have children, celebrate the goodness of life and the kindness of our God.

When you come to know God, a new affection takes hold of you—the love of God and your response to God. When a person recognizes that he or she is loved unconditionally by God, that is a transforming moment—me, known and loved by God!

This profound sense of being loved and then loving in return begins to change your life. The way you live, how and where you work, and your daily activity may change gradually. But these changes will occur because of your love for God and God's love for you.

Think of this love as "the transformative power of a new affection"!

VI

Q. Can you sum up in one sentence what it means to be a Christian?

A. One sentence?

To be a Christian is to have a personal relationship with God through Jesus Christ that changes us from rebellious antagonists of God into friends and seekers after God's will.

VII

Q. How do we reach out to God?

A. The shortest reach is a simple prayer: "O God, I desire you and your will for my life."

We also meet God by letting God reach out to us. When we read the story of Jesus, God often reaches out to us through the words Jesus spoke.

Sometimes God reaches out to us through others. Find a genuine Christian and talk with her; share your feelings and hunger. Let yourself be available to God in the conversation.

God reaches us when we stop, pay attention, and listen for God.

We hope you will both reach out in prayer and attend to God's reaching out to you in scripture, in others, and in your own waiting.

VIII

Q. When I talk to God, how do I know if it is God telling me what to do and not my own conscience?

A. We are all afraid it's just us, aren't we? Afraid we're talking to ourselves?

When you ask God about a certain direction or choice, listen for ideas to come into your mind. When they come, do they sound like a negative parent or like Jesus Christ? If it sounds like a scolding parent, entertain a question about this communication being from God.

Your conscience is helpful, if it has been educated properly. The problem is that often we have contamination left over from the past, and we need to purge our conscience of bad data.

If the communication comes from God, it will be clear, persistent, and persuasive over a period of time.

Don't give up on this personal transaction with God. You'll soon learn the language of God.

IX

Q. How does God respond to our prayers?

A. The first and simplest way is, "Yes," "No," or "Wait." These three responses encompass most of God's answers to us.

We suspect that you are asking a deeper question, such as "How does our prayer affect God or induce God to act?" We can only speculate, because none of us knows the inside answer of how and why God does what God does.

But we suspect that God ordained prayer as a means of relationship with us. God desired us to come into the divine presence with our needs, desires, and hopes. Many of these lie outside the bounds of our ability to achieve, and we need help from beyond.

God may have so ordered creation that human desiring and hungering form part of the structure of reality, so that we participate with God in bringing God's rule to the affairs of the world.

Also, it is possible that since everything is connected to everything, God's Spirit may even flow through our desires and imaginations as we pray for other people.

Followers of Jesus count on a loving God who invites us to participate with God in creation, the correction of evil, and the building of community.

What an incredible gift to be invited to join in the creativity of God! We hope these different speculations will encourage you to venture into the mystery of God's amazing action in the world.

X

Q. When you've prayed and believe that you have an answer but you're blocked at almost every turn, does that mean you misunderstood?

A. Having obstacles in your face may indicate that you have misunderstood the guidance of the Lord, but not necessarily. God does use "closed doors" to show you the way not to go.

Obstacles may be a test to your obedience and your faith. When obstacles come, persist in the direction God has called you. Explore every avenue; walk through every open door; knock on closed doors to see if they will open.

In the time of your seeking to obey the call of God, keep praying that God will make clear to you what you are to do. When all pathways are blocked, tell the Lord that you are willing to go forward but that you cannot open the door. If God wants you to move, God must open the door.

Commit your way to the Lord; rest in faith; and know that nothing is too difficult for God. If your call continues, rest in the confidence that at the right moment the door will open. Until God acts, you are pleasing God by your trust in God's love and power.

XI

Q. How do I know if I am on the right path in my search?

A. The answer, of course, is determined by what you are searching for!

We assume that you mean God. When you try to find out more about God, when you meet with folk who know God, and when you see your life changing in love and compassion, becoming more like Jesus Christ's, you may assume that you are on the right track. Usually, people on the way to God begin to show the character of Jesus.

If all this checks out, pay attention to the deepest desires of your heart. Take seriously the impulses and intuitions that come to you. Sometimes God speaks to us through them.

But you may also be on the right path when it seems that nothing is changing in you. All you see is failure, struggle, and starting over. This makes you wonder if you are on the right track and if God is noticing. It may be that God is very much in this struggle with you. One question is essential: Does God matter to you? Do knowing God and doing God's will matter? If God matters, you are on the journey!

We also think it is good to check with trusted Christian friends about the direction of your life. For example, share your search with a friend; reveal to him or her what you are discovering, and then ask for feedback.

Do you feel at peace in your present direction? Follow your peace!

XII

Q. All I feel is numb. I am driven by my job, husband, a teenager, house responsibilities, a yard to keep, and a large extended family. How do I get to a more sane life?

A. Slow down! Prioritize your responsibilities.

If you feel numb, you probably recognize that you are in a rut. You are living from memory, like a tape recording. You tend to do things by rote, without being aware and present to your life.

Stop! Interrupt your routine! Pay attention to what you are doing—even the simplest thing, such as getting out of bed, walking to the bathroom, choosing your clothes for the day. Attend to what goes on inside yourself as you make these moves.

Again and again throughout the day, return to the present moment. Feel your numbness dissolve. When other tiny feelings, such as gratitude for your spouse and children, pop into your mind, cultivate the thought and the feelings that flow from it

Keep attending your life until you "feel" again.

We believe a life lived in awareness is a sane life. Living in awareness breaks the monotony of a preprogrammed life and liberates your consciousness to experience God and new dimensions of your being.

XIII

Q. How do you know you are closer to God?

A. The way you put this question suggests that you are concerned with growth. If you had said "close" to God, we would have thought that you often felt far away from God and that you wanted to feel close.

But you ask about closer! The sense of the presence of God comes to us in two ways: through reason and through emotion. When you examine your life and discover that God's will is being done in your life through right living, service to others, and a spirit of forgiveness, you may conclude that you are on the right track. This comes to us through a reasonable reflection on our behavior.

In addition, notice the things that matter to you. When God matters to you, when you consider God's desire and intention for you, this suggests that you are in relationship with God and that you are focused in God's direction. When you notice your love for God growing, we would say that you are closer to God.

Interestingly, the saints seem to agree that the closer we get to God, the farther we often feel from God. This paradoxical experience might give us pause.

P.S.: Beware of making "closeness to God" either an end in itself or a self-centered craving.

XIV

Q. Is there a sin that can't be forgiven?

A. The Bible speaks of a sin "against the Holy Spirit" for which persons do not receive forgiveness in this world or in the world to come. Bible scholars have debated through the ages about what this sin could be.

We believe that this refers to persons who have an opportunity to receive God's love but persist in rebellion and self-will. Even when they hear the truth about God, they refuse it. After refusing God's offer over and over and over again, they finally become fixed in their rejection. This rejection becomes unpardonable not because God is angry but because the person has become frozen in his or her rejection.

If you are worried that you may have committed the "unpardonable sin," your concern offers strong evidence that you have not. Rather, look upon your concern about the unpardonable sin as God's way of getting your attention.

XV

Q. I've had times when I felt very close to God, but when I try to go back to that closeness, it's not the same. How do I feel the closeness of God again?

A. How many of us have had this experience!

The desire to recover a past experience is very normal, but it cannot be done. Recall the experience of closeness in the past, appreciate it, and release it to God. Do not make an idol of it.

A fixation on the past blinds you to the new things God is doing in your life or the new idea that God may wish to speak to you. Come to the present! Be present to God in the context of your life today.

Remember, you can't find God in the past or in the future. God is present in the present moment. God is in the here and now.

You often miss the real presence in this moment because you have decided how God comes to you, and because God does not come in the expected manner, you miss the real way in which God is present to you now. Forget the past, and come to the present. Be present to the present moment. Surprise!

XVI

Q. Does God just let the world go? Is everything chance? Or does God intervene in life?

A. No! Decidedly, God does not let the world go! In the most radical sense of "letting the world go," we would experience nothing of the care and activity of God in the world. This idea of God letting the world go is an old Deist notion. Like a clockmaker, God created the world, wound it up, and turned it loose on its own. This suggests that God is an absent and careless creator.

Nothing is left to chance. In the field of human freedom, God acts with persuasive power to bring about the divine purpose in the world. The purpose of God that functions in history does so through God's initiative and power, but God does not violate our personhood.

Thus, our answer to the last part of your question: yes, God does intervene in our lives, but with such respect that our personhood is not violated, nor is freedom destroyed. In this response, you see our efforts to struggle with the ambiguity caused by the interface of human freedom and divine sovereignty.

XVII

Q. When you are in a "dry period" in your relationship with God, how do you get it going again?

A. This is a good question because it is so common and a situation we botch quite often. Of first importance is our evaluation of the "dry" place. Most of us evaluate this experience negatively by wondering where we have failed or what we have done wrong so that our sense of God seems distant or nonexistent. By wandering in this direction, we are easily led into self-doubt, depression, and feelings of hopelessness. At the end of this road lies the pit of doubt concerning God's love and continuous care for us. Along this pathway, we also begin to look for ways to resist the dryness, overcome the problem, and escape from the desert.

We believe the effort to escape the dryness plays right into the hands of our enemy. Satan is pleased to see us traversing this territory, because it leads to self-deprecating thoughts and ambivalent attitudes.

Evaluate your dryness from another perspective. Think of dryness as an expression of God's love. A lover can leave you because she is angry and seeks to punish you, but a lover can also stay away to test your love or to let it grow stronger. Suppose you think of God as asking through the dryness, "How much do you love me?"

If Jesus is the "water of life," to be in a dry place forces you to realize how very much you need water, how much you miss water, and how essential water is for life. This profound awareness makes you long for the presence of God and appreciate it more deeply when you are immersed in it.

To look at dryness in this manner means that you should turn toward your dryness, not away from it; that you should embrace it rather than avoid it; and that you should look for the presence and call of God in your dryness, instead of wanting to get away from it.

Dryness is not so dry after all. The river of God is present in it!

XVIII

Q. Why was I born? What's the point to my life?

A. Come on. Give us a break.

We have enough problems trying to figure out why *we* were born. And what is the point of *our* lives? Must we take on yours, too?

Nevertheless, try one of these answers: "You were born to love God and to enjoy God forever!" Or: "You were born to fulfill God's will by discovering the gifts you have been given and using them to the fullest for the good of the most people."

The point in our lives is to discern our gifts, our pathway, and to obey the call of God implicitly. This clear focus for your life is what it is about!

CONCLUSION

– – – – – –

Words of Counsel for Today's Seekers

We are very much aware that in one sense of the word, all of us are seekers, even those who have found. Followers of Jesus continue to search because no matter how long they have been following him, they realize that they are still beginners. There is so much to learn; there is so far to go.

But there are seekers who, in the most basic sense, are just beginning to discover who Jesus Christ is and what it means to be in a personal relationship with him. Setting forth the Jesus story has been our effort to assist persons in their knowledge of Jesus and what it means to be one of his followers today.

After reading *The Jesus Story* and following some of the suggestions we have made along the way, you may still have unsatisfied hungers and unanswered questions. We have no way of knowing what your assessment of Jesus may be at this point in your quest. We hope this brief narrative of his life and accomplishments has stimulated you to inquire further how you may learn more about him or how you might actually become more aware of his living presence in your life. When this question becomes a personal issue, we suspect that you are already very near the divine presence. Actually, the question itself suggests that the presence has become active in your consciousness, making Jesus a matter of concern for you.

If there exists in your awareness a persistent interest, where do you suppose the interest came from? What sustains it?

Permit us, for the moment, to assume that you would like to make further inquiry into the person of Jesus Christ. How can you continue? To be quite honest, you are more likely to deepen your awareness of the presence in some settings than in others. The initiatives that you can take will likely increase your awareness and your knowledge.

Since we are not there to talk with you about these, here are several ways to explore further the meaning of Jesus for today. Consider the ones that might be helpful to you.

FURTHER EXPLORATIONS

- Make a definite commitment to a serious inquiry over the next sixty days, with the resolve that you will read again *The Jesus Story* in no more than two sittings.
- Keep a journal of your insights and your experiences during this sixty-day period. (A journal is simply a record of experiences with God, and it may be a spiral notebook, a computer file, or a bound book of sorts.) What strange things happened to you? What new feelings about yourself and God do you experience? Who comes into your life who can help you on this journey? Notice and record experiences like these.
- Look for a vital Christian community—a church. Not every church will automatically be a good place for you to look for the presence of Christ. Seek one that seems eager and unembarrassed to speak about Jesus. Look for one in which the leader speaks about Jesus and invites the congregation to love, worship, and obey him.
- Schedule a day to spend close to nature, alone. Take a trip to the mountains, the beach, or the forests. Look at the earth with its beauty and majesty, and wonder about its beginning, its purpose, and your place in it. Attend other thoughts that come to you spontaneously during the day. Be sure to write your reflections in your journal.
- Begin to pay attention to different aspects of the culture in which you live. In music, drama, films, arts, and literature there are numerous hints of the divine presence, especially those expressions that deal with persistent human dilemmas and hungers. The presence appears incognito in the culture but is definitely at work, and we have found that the lenses to our glasses have been adjusted by our contact with Jesus, so that we are better able to see it.
- When you attend a service of worship in a Christian community, pay special attention to the reading and teaching of the Bible. The Spirit of Christ speaks through these ancient words

and human efforts to speak his word in a contemporary setting. He often illuminates our imagination with the words and images that we hear.

- Look for Jesus' ministry in other aspects of the culture. The Bible describes Jesus as showing compassion, forgiveness, and reconciling persons who have been separated from one another. Knowing that this is what he is doing today, try to find his presence in acts of compassion and reconciliation among persons in our culture.

- When you attend a church that celebrates Holy Communion (the Eucharist or the Lord's Supper), if you have been baptized, take the bread and the wine. He is present in this bread and wine. Think about receiving him into yourself as you ingest these natural elements made sacred by consecration.

- Another place that you are likely to experience the living Christ is in the fellowship of a worshiping community. In the church, Christ is present in the love and worship of the people; in scripture, Christ is present in the words, making them alive in our minds; and in the Holy Communion, he is present in natural elements of bread and wine, making them bearers of his presence to us.

- Should you attend a baptism, recall the meaning of your own baptism. Whether you fully realize it or not, by baptism you were made part of the body of Jesus Christ. If you have not been baptized, listen to the words the minister says and think what being baptized would mean to you.

- One of the most direct ways to meet Christ is through prayer. No doubt you have prayed at some time in your life. It may have been uninformed and self-serving, but it was prayer nevertheless. Begin your prayer by thinking about all the things that have been given you, things for which you had no responsibility, and give thanks to God. There is much more to prayer than this, but thanksgiving is the place to begin.

- Among all your acquaintances, who knows the most about Jesus Christ? Make an appointment to talk with this person. Share with him or her the journey you have been making for the past months. Discuss questions that have been bothering you.

- Review the notes you have been taking over the past month. What have you discovered about Jesus? What are the major questions that you have? In what places or experiences have you been most aware of his presence? What are the next steps that you will take in this quest?

Should you be interested in writing to either of us, we will gladly respond to your questions. Permitting us to share in your journey would be a gift to us.

Ben Johnson   Brant Baker
Columbia Theological Seminary   First Presbyterian Church
Box 520   161 N. Mesa Drive
Decatur, GA 30031   Mesa, AZ 85201